Top
Islands
OF THE WORLD

Top
Islands
OF THE WORLD

First published in 2006 by New Holland Publishers
LONDON • CAPE TOWN • SYDNEY • AUCKLAND
www.newhollandpublishers.com

86 Edgware Road, London, W2 2EA, United Kingdom

80 McKenzie Street, Cape Town, 8001, South Africa

14 Aquatic Drive, Frenchs Forest, NSW 2086, Australia

218 Lake Road, Northcote, Auckland, New Zealand

ISBN 1 84537 178 X

Publishing managers	Claudia dos Santos, Simon Pooley
Commissioning editor	Alfred LeMaitre
Editor	Leizel Brown, Rod Baker
Designer	Christelle Marais
Cartographer	Elaine Fick
Illustrator	Louwra Marais
Picture researchers	Karla Kik, Tamlyn Beaumont-Thomas
Production	Myrna Collins
Proofreader	Tricia Shannon

Reproduction by Resolution Colour (pty) Ltd, Cape Town, South Africa
Printed and bound in Singapore by Tien Wah Press (Pte) Ltd

10 9 8 7 6 5 4 3 2

MAP SYMBOLS

✈	AIRPORT	▲	PEAK
⤨	BEACH	■	POINT OF INTEREST
∩	CAVE		REEF
⤵	DIVING		
┄┄►	FERRY ROUTE	A850	ROUTE NUMBER
──	MAJOR ROAD	♂	SNORKELING
──	OTHER ROAD	○	TOWN SYMBOL

Page 1 *Stromboli, home to one of Europe's most active volcanoes.*

Page 2 - 3 *Duntulm Bay, on the island of Skye, takes its name from the nearby ruined castle of the same name.*

This page *Mauritius, a jewel of the Indian Ocean.*

Contents page *We are drawn to the sea and the world's islands.*

contents

Introduction

WILLIAM GRAY

'Truly prepossessing was our first view,' wrote explorer Richard Burton when he visited Zanzibar in the mid 1800s. 'Earth, sea and sky all seemed wrapped in a soft and sensuous repose...' But not all early travellers waxed lyrical about the island known locally as Unguja, lying 40km (25 miles) off the coast of Tanzania. In 1866, David Livingstone turned his nose up and wrote: 'The stench is quite horrible. At night it is so gross and crass, one might cut a slice and manure the garden with it. It might be called 'Stinkibar' rather than Zanzibar.'

The fact that one man's paradise can be another man's compost pile only serves to emphasize the dilemma faced in selecting the world's 'top islands' for this book. When it comes to Zanzibar, however, I have no hesitation in siding with Burton. It was late October when I visited the legendary spice island and the first whisper of the northeast monsoon scuffed the sea, streaking flecks of white across its azure surface. From the vantage of a single-propeller Cessna, I could make out several dhows far below, their lateen sails taut before the breeze, glowing like the wings of swans in the glancing light of dawn. Ahead, Zanzibar cowered beneath towering thunderclouds. As we began our descent, the Cessna was rocked by turbulence and, in my own flight of fancy, I imagined that we were struggling back in time — crossing a threshold from the present into 2000 years of history.

Islands are enigmatic and irresistible. They have always captivated travellers, from ocean-wandering Polynesians and Arabian traders to great navigators like Magellan and Columbus. Of course, there are no longer any islands awaiting discovery — humans have laid claim to the remotest speck and mapped each one from space. But still they fill our daydreams as places to escape the hectic cycle of modern-day life. No matter how many people have made landfall before you, there is always that tantalizing and pioneering sense of exploration when you travel to an island.

It was during a particularly reluctant dawn that I first sighted the Shetland Islands. Storm clouds slouched on the horizon and the sea was grey and languid — more like bath water than the notorious confluence of the Atlantic Ocean and North Sea. During the long night's voyage from Aberdeen, the ferry's windows had frosted over with salt grime and many of the passengers had ventured out on deck for a glimpse of land. Fair Isle, the most southerly of the Shetlands, was little more than a fog-bound smudge on our port side, but it still sent a ripple of excitement along the deck rails. As we continued north towards the main group of islands, a swirling procession of gannets and fulmars followed in our wake. Soon the cliffs of Sumburgh Head were slipping past and we were nuzzling into Lerwick harbour on the largest of the islands, known as Mainland. I turned from the railing to join the scrummage on the car deck, but it seemed that not everyone was enthusiastic about our arrival. 'Trees — that's what I really miss,' said a homeward-bound local standing next to me. 'Trees would be nice – and Woolworths. I miss Woolworths too.' As you will discover in the following pages, islands are quirky, complex places, rich in their unique blends of history, culture, landscape and wildlife. Our 27 top islands rise metaphorically above countless others that pepper our seas and oceans. Some, like Kauai, are miniature worlds, complete with an incredible diversity of scenery, ranging from mountains and canyons to rain-forests and swamps. Rhodes, meanwhile, is Greece in microcosm where relics from the Classical, Roman, Byzantine, Frankish and Ottoman periods are condensed from great swathes of history. A few islands even have celebrity status. Kefalonia was catapulted into the limelight by Louis de Bernieres's novel and subsequent movie, *Captain Corelli's Mandolin* – but did you know that *Jurassic Park* and *Raiders of the Lost Ark* were filmed partly on Kauai? Or that Robert Louis Stevenson, author of *Treasure Island*, used the Tahitian jewel of Bora Bora to feed his imagination?

From the well-known and popular holiday isles of Capri, Malta and Jersey to the less familiar Rügen, Korcula and Lord Howe Island, chances are you will find your personal favourites in this book – plus a good spattering of others to keep those desert island daydreams alive. During the last 14 years working as a travel writer, I have been fortunate enough to visit dozens of islands around the world but, judging by this book's content, there are still plenty to add to my wish list.

I love the way that 'small island worlds' force you to slow down and appreciate subtleties and quirky details. On a recent voyage around Svalbard in the Arctic, for example, a few minutes of beachcombing turned up an old Russian gas mask and an assortment of shoes, all of them right-footed. In the Scottish Hebrides I have spent many hours watching a rising tide nuzzle rocks drizzled with honey-coloured seaweed, each rhythmic swell chuckling through the heaped piles of kelp, massaging them to life until they are twitching, swirling and cavorting with the sea – playing otter-tricks with my mind.

Something else that always fascinated me about islands is how they are colonized. My first serious island escapade was a five-week stint on a coral cay 60km (37 miles) from the nearest mainland at the southern tip of Australia's Great Barrier Reef. The island was so small I could stroll around its perimeter in 20 minutes – and yet it was thickly forested and inhabited by tens of thousands of birds.

Fourth century theologian and philosopher St Augustine concluded that while birds could reach an island by flying there, many of the other creatures, and certainly all of the plants, must have been transported by angels under divine command. Augustine died long before the exploration of the great oceans began, and he would perhaps have been amazed to learn of the existence of verdant mid-oceanic islands such as Fiji and Réunion. Today we understand far more about the mechanisms of dispersal – from the salt-resistant coconut that can withstand four months floating at sea to the myriad insects riding high-atmosphere winds in a bid to expand their ranges.

Nevertheless, the chances of making landfall on an island are slim. And even for the few that do make it, there is a high probability that colonization will fail due to a shortage of food, shelter or breeding partners. For those that do beat the odds, however, an island presents a world of opportunities. In Hawaii, for example, evolution has forged over 40 species of honeycreeper, each one perfectly adapted to exploit a vacant ecological niche. Charles Darwin observed a similar example of this so-called 'adaptive radiation' in a family of finches on the Galápagos Islands. Other island colonists have become giants or lost the ability to fly.

Evolving into something highly specialized that is endemic to one or two islands may sound like paradise found, but what these species hadn't counted on was the subsequent arrival of a creature that, on the face of it, should never have succeeded as an island colonist. It was a large mammal, the sort of thing that should have con-demned itself by quickly outstripping the limited natural resources of an island. But as Tom Hanks demonstrated in the blockbuster *Castaway*, ingenuity is the key to human survival. So when the ancestors of the Polynesians began dispersing through the islands of the Pacific around 5000 years ago they stepped ashore not as vulnerable colonists but as well-equipped travellers. Their sea-lore involved memorizing 'star paths' to help them navigate by night, and studying distant clouds that changed colour as they passed over yet-to-be-discovered islands. During their epic voyages they relied on the sea for food, but their canoes were also stocked with seeds, cuttings, chickens, pigs and everything else they needed for sustaining a new life.

By the time the Polynesians had completed their conquest of the Pacific (around AD750), islands throughout the Indian and Atlantic oceans had also been colonized. Indigenous wildlife reeled from the impact of the new arrivals. Flightless birds were hopelessly ill-equipped to escape hunters, while coastal forests were cleared to make way for crops. Today, many islands are precious reservoirs of biodiversity, providing strongholds for some of the world's rarest plants and animals.

Following in the wake of the early colonists came traders, whalers, missionaries, fishermen, pirates, slaves, shipwreck survivors, opportunists and escapists – a colour-ful cast of characters that has laid the cultural bedrock for many of the islands featured in this book.

Ultimately, however, the lure of islands is not so much their wildlife, culture or history as the subtle pleasures of being somewhere remote and detached. There is nothing more invigorating or liberating than to shun the mainland for a spell on an island.

Previous page *Santorini can go from being ghostly and desolate to being an exqui-site island with bright blue skies, good restaurants and cafés.*

Opposite *Spectacular scenery, crystal clear waters and its wonderful climate all combine to make the Italian island of Capri a major tourist attraction.*

Above *The present-day tranquility of the Bay of Sami, with the island of Ithaca in*

the distance, belies its often turbulent history in bygone centuries.

Europe and the Mediterranean

Capri

ZOE ROSS

The jewel-like waters of the Tyrrhenian Sea surrounding the small island of Capri are a major contributor to it being one of Italy's most beautiful attractions – no small feat in a country overrun with natural and man-made glories. Just 5.5km (3.4 miles) off the Sorrentine Peninsula and 27km (17 miles) from Naples, Capri, unlike its 'big sister' Sicily, with its shady streets and shady reputation, has come to symbolize glamour and the true *dolce vita* – a sun-baked playground for generations of hedonists.

It was the Greeks who first inhabited this 6.5km (4-mile) long, 3km (1.8-mile) wide island, but it was the Romans who really put it on the map. Most notable among them was Emperor Tiberius, who secured the island for himself in AD27 and built 12 villas across its landscape, each one dedicated to an Olympian god. Escaping the political machinations of Rome, Tiberius used Capri as a retreat on which to indulge his sexual pleasures. Legend has it that those who

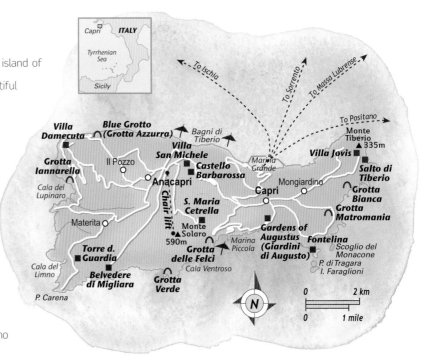

refused his advances were thrown from the island's craggy cliffs at a point still known as *Salto di Tiberio* (Tiberius's Leap). The sensual reputation thus begun, Capri has remained an idyll for pleasure-seekers ever since. In the early 20th century, it lured writers such as Graham Greene and Maxim Gorky to its shores; in the 1960s it was a haven of the jet set, including the quintessence of glamour, Jackie Onassis.

Today the atmosphere may be a little calmer and less iniquitous, but Capri still remains a very 'grown up' holiday retreat. Its limited size, vertiginous landscape and lack of sandy beaches have been its saviour from the fate of so many Mediterranean resorts. Despite some 17km (10.5 miles) of coastline, the seafront at such places as Marina Piccola and Fontelina is small, pebbly and, in the case of the latter, accessible only on foot via a steep hillside descent. But people don't generally come to Capri to sunbathe. Its attraction lies in its lifestyle.

There are two towns on the island, the eponymous Capri in the east and, in the west, the smaller Anacapri. Capri is the hub and the place to flash only very serious cash. The streets are lined with a roll-call of designer names, while its hotel terraces drip with millionaires. At night, the central square Piazza Umberto I is the scene of the classic *passeggiata*, the nighttime stroll so beloved of Italians as an opportunity to dress up and catch up, to flirt and to pose. To miss this would be to miss the point. Unlike so much of Italy, Capri is far more about attitude than art.

From the town of Capri, too, there are stunning views of the mainland and of one of the island's most favoured sights, I Faraglioni. These three eroded limestone rocks rise out of the sea like imperial vanguards, over 100m (328ft) tall, and are home to the rare native 'blue lizards' that scuttle across the wave-lapped stones.

Sadly, none of the island's Roman structures survive in anything close to their entirety, but on the northeastern tip remains can still be seen of the most famous and largest Roman residence, Villa Jovis. What was once the main base of the infamous Tiberius still displays remnants of cisterns and thermal bathing areas, as well as outlines of grand halls and the emperor's quarters. A viewing platform is now located at the point where Tiberius purportedly threw reluctant lovers 300m (984ft) down to the sea, but belying its terrifying history, this is now a tranquil spot offering a magnificent view

Right *Boatmen escort visitors through the narrow entrance of the Blue Grotto* (Grotta Azzurra), *one of the major attractions on the island of Capri.*

Opposite *The breathtaking view from Monte Solaro, the highest point of Capri, includes three limestone rock formations, I Faraglioni, rising out from the sea.*

of the Bay of Naples and the azure waters below. Villa Damecuta, on the opposite side of the island, is another Roman villa that has partly survived the ravages of time, but again the draw here is the view. On a clear day – of which there are many – you can see the looming hulk of Mt Vesuvius towering over the mainland. It's believed that the villa was abandoned when Vesuvius erupted violently in AD79, completely devastating Pompeii and burying it in ash – archaeologists discovered the villa's ruins also cloaked in volcanic ash, presumably carried by wind across the bay.

With a landscape made up of crags and caves there are numerous grottoes on the island, but it is the eerie cerulean light of the Blue Grotto (*Grotta Azzurra*) that draws the largest crowds. Wealthy Romans delighted in this cool and peaceful setting – locals avoided it, believing it was inhabited by evil spirits – but it was its rediscovery in 1826 that sparked a wave of tourism here that has never waned. Its appeal, like all the world's natural wonders, is due to a simple geological development – an eroded hole in the cave wall, above and below sea level, allows a shaft of sunlight into the darkness, refracting light onto its magnificent blue waters. As if still unnerved by the interior serenity, a group of eccentric boatmen are on hand to ferry visitors through the low entrance and fill the cavernous space with the reverberating sound of their operatic singing.

In contrast to the stylish bustle of Capri Town, Anacapri is an altogether quieter place, foregoing designer names in favour of local products, including *limoncello*, the region's liqueur. The whitewashed lanes, offset by jasmine trees and morning glory, whirr with the sound of Vespas and the gesticulating hussle and bustle of daily life. The area is dominated by Monte Solaro, Capri's highest point, and in summer a chair lift carries visitors on a precarious but exhilarating ride to the 590m (1935ft) summit, skimming the pine forests down below.

In Anacapri is the Villa San Michele, a palatial home built on the site of one of Tiberius's 12 villas by a 19th-century Swedish doctor named Axel Munthe. The house itself is largely devoted to the works of Munthe and the few Roman finds excavated from the grounds, but the real attraction here is the garden, where walkways shaded with hibiscus and Cypress trees have been landscaped into a modern-day Eden. A cloistered semicircular path looks out over the bay, at the end of which is the Sphinx Parapet where a stone version of the mythical creature looks down over the activities of the main port. Touching the Egyptian statue with your left hand, so the legend goes, will make all your wishes come true.

Munthe wasn't the only northern European to fall under the spell of Capri. Around the same period, on the other side of the island, the German industrialist Baron Krupp re-landscaped another Roman site into a bucolic garden setting. But once satisfied with his work, Krupp generously donated the haven to the people as a public park. The people, in turn, re-named it the Gardens of Augustus, in honour of the original Roman resident.

In large part, the success of these formal gardens is thanks to the fertile limestone soil that makes the whole island so abundant

Above left *Piazza Umberto I, more commonly known as La Piazzetta, lies at the heart of Capri Town – here the visitor can dress up and join in the* passeggiata.
Left *Rows of fishing boats line the shore of Marina Grande, ready to take visitors on trips along the island's coastline.*
Opposite *A spectacular view from Villa San Michele of Marina Grande and, in the distance, the Sorrentine Peninsula on the Italian mainland can also be seen.*

in greenery. At every turn the landscape offers up trees burdened with lemons, olives or pomegranates, the intoxicating aroma of jasmine blooms and herb bushes, vines swaying in the breeze and the crimson bougainvillea flowers that never fail to lift the spirit. Add to the palette the turquoise waters lapping the rocky shore, and the whole island becomes a natural masterpiece of artistic achievement.

Capri is a one-off in its southern European setting. Sure, there are tourists — plenty of them. But there are no overcrowded beaches, with parasols lined up cheek by jowl. Nor are there high-rise hotels, thumping nightlife or exuberant kids' clubs. What there is is style, a soft-focus elegance and, above all, a true sense of escape from the chaos of the outside world that, in reality, lies only 40 minutes away across the bay.

The Aeolian Islands

FIONA NICHOLS

*N*amed for the Greek God of Wind, Aeolus, the Aeolian archipelago is indeed windy. Scattered like a three-pointed star in the Tyrrhenian Sea just north of Sicily, the islands sheltered invading warships and harboured trade vessels for some 6000 years. It is thought that Homer's famous *Odyssey* was in part based on the myths inspired by these islands. Didn't Odysseus take refuge in a walled village, such as the Bronze Age settlement on Alicudi? Could Roman god Vulcan's fiery forge not be the cauldron atop Vulcano? And the monstrous one-eyed Cyclops slain by our hero, Odysseus, was he not perhaps one of Vulcan's feared smiths?

However melodic the island names – Stromboli, Vulcano, Lipari, Panarea, Salina, Filicudi and Alicudi – they mask a darker side, for these seven Italian isles were born of natural disaster: one million years ago volcanic eruptions

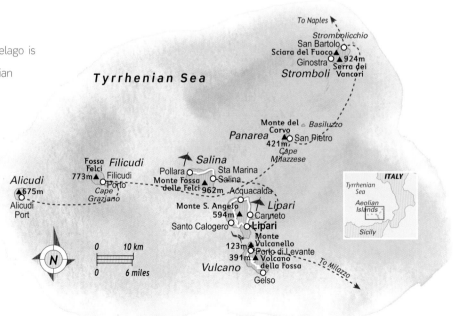

thrust the northern islands skyward. Much later, the southern islands broke the sea's surface, while the others still remained submerged.

Two of the isles – Vulcano and Stromboli – spluttering and smoking, are far from calm today and yet, amazingly, people elect to live in their shadow, inspired by a love of their isles balanced by an eye wary of the smouldering peaks. Indeed, if neighbouring Mt Etna claims the title of Europe's most active volcano, Stromboli comes a close second. In the Aeolian Islands the elements – earth, wind, fire and water – meet with spectacular results.

The way to explore these islands is by water and, although sandy beaches are few, swimming in the translucent waters is wonderful even in tiny harbours and close to pebbly shores. A behemoth of a car ferry trundles around the islands, leaving Milazzo on the northern coast of Sicily and finishing its journey at Naples, hours before turning around and retracing its path. There are also smaller ferries and hydrofoils that skim the surface in half the time, but to arrive leisurely in the company of the hardy islanders is far more appropriate.

Vulcano is just over 20km (12.5 miles) from Sicily's north coast. This is not the largest island, but at 22km² (8.6sq.miles) it is closest to the mainland. In geological terms it is a 'baby', for it is believed to have been formed only 136,000 years ago; the smaller Vulcanello to the north of Vulcano, joined to it by an isthmus, only came into existence in 183BC. For the Greeks and Romans it must have been an awesome event. Formerly known as Hierà (the Sacred One), its name later changed to Vulcano.

The ferry slips along its eastern side, where steep, dark cliffs rise from indigo depths. A ring of thick, green vegetation clings like a dark green beard to the upper slopes, while cube-like houses speckle the flatter land, which is home to some of the island's 8000 inhabitants. Way above, wispy plumes rise from the 391m (1300ft) peak, Volcano della Fossa.

Vulcano has not exploded for over 100 years and so is considered dormant, but those pungent fumeroles – the sign of cooling magma deep in the mountain – still release sulphuric gases. If you have a head for heights and can tolerate the bad smell, it should take you about two hours to climb up from the main village of Porto di Levante and examine these first hand. Hissing and spurting steam, the ground around is thick in yellow sulphuric matter.

Above right *Stromboli volcano is active, and even though the inhabitants are under constant threat of it erupting at any time, they choose to live on the island.*
Right *Canneto is the main powdered pumice beach of Lipari, and popular with tourists visiting the island.*
Opposite *Once called Hierà (the Sacred One), also Termessa or Terrasia, Vulcano is an island well known for its natural hot springs.*

The words 'Vulcano' and 'Stromboli' have entered into the English language — both gave their names to two of the four main types of volcanic activity: Strombolian (persistent and moderately explosive with periodic lava flows) and Vulcanian (a projection of magma and water, cinders and lava flow). The other two are Plinean and Hawaiian.

The spa-loving Romans flocked to Vulcano for its hot waters, black sand and volcanic mud, and you can still wallow, for short periods of time, in these amazingly hot waters as a therapeutic cure for rheumatism and arthritis, or just for the fun of it. As the ferry leaves Porto di Levante bound for Lipari, black-bodied tourists wave enthusiastically from the volcanic sands near Vulcanello. In the distance, a boat awaits scuba divers who have been exploring the rich fauna in the warm sea channel between Lipari and Vulcano.

At 38.6km² (15sq.miles), Lipari is the main island and the administrative centre for all except Salina. It is home to over 10,000 inhabitants, and has been known to man for well over 5000 years. The volcanic earth abounds with the metal alum and shiny black obsidian, which was essential to our ancestors in tool-making; feather-light pumice stone was used like sandpaper though today it's also used in cosmetics and in the process of ageing blue jeans!

Lipari has the air of a prosperous Italian port: bright, colourful and vibrant. From the early Bronze Age until the age of Sicilian Baroque it played a pivotal role in the wave of colonizing invasions and was at the centre of Tyrrhenian trade. Nowadays, rainbow-coloured fishing boats nudge noses with flashy cruisers and ferries. Back on terra firma pedestrian Via Garibaldi pulses with human life. Outside stucco-coloured restaurants and shops vivid red Stromboli ceramic bowls, bottles of local wine and heady liquors from mandarins or almonds, skeins of knotted garlic, dried biscotti and chains of chillies dangling like Chinese firecrackers invite you through dark doorways to cool interiors and more merchandise.

The highlight of Lipari, housed in one of the buildings on the erstwhile Acropolis, is the Museo Archelogico Eoliano, an archeological collection that traces the islands' rich history. Of supremely high quality, with excellent labelling, it's eons away from other dust-catching provincial museums. Artefacts dating from its Neolithic and Bronze Age settlements document the Greek, Carthaginian and Roman periods of colonization, relate the Muslim invasions, and then take you through the Christian efforts to reclaim the islands 1000 years ago, to the 16th century rebuilding and repopulating when the island's history paralleled that of Sicily and Naples.

Although the obsidian tools are ingenious, it's the pottery and perfectly intact amphorae that catch your breath. Mycenean influences in some ceramics confirm the breadth of Aeolian trade routes. There are even Classical era tombs preserved forever when Lipari's Monte Chirica smothered a necropolis with ash. Thanks to volcanoes and myriad shipwrecks, the museum has a world-class collection.

Lipari has some 26km (16 miles) of roads encircling the isle which means that you can hop on or off a bus at the pumice beach at Canneto or Acquacalda,

Above *This tiny shop, with its outside displays of vegetables and chillies that are hung above the doorway, is typical of Lipari .*

Right *This vase which is housed in the Archeological Museum expresses, in its unique design on the rim, the labours of the Greek god Hercules.*

Opposite *An aerial view overlooking the Old Town on the main island and administrative centre, Lipari.*

or even stop off at the pumice quarries and Roman-built baths at Santo Calogero. At the centre of the archipelago lies saddle-shaped Salina, named for the salt flat that was once prized for its wind-dried salt. It's a verdant island, just 26km^2 (10sq.miles) in size and rising to 962m (3200ft) at the peak of its perfect cone, Monte Fossa delle Felci. Salina is unique as it has abundant water supplies and as such is the garden of the Aeolian isles, lending its locals a less challenging lifestyle.

Salina's character emerges as soon as you set foot on the island. Homes are fashioned from simple but colourful cubes of stucco and Rome-chic tourists are scarcer. Red grapes are cultivated, sun-dried and squeezed into heady Malvasia wine; citrus, capers and olive groves tame the higher reaches stretching to the chestnut forests.

Life must have been agreeable here for millennia for excavations reveal remains of a Bronze Age village and bits of Roman houses. But Salina has a certain familiarity.

Those almost vertical, layered cliffs (home to the island's falcons and shearwaters) towering over the pebbly beach at Pollara figured often in the delightful 1994 film, *Il Postino*, the Postman. Here too are the fields of yellow broom, ferns and bracken, *felce*, after which Monte Fossa delle Felci, is named.

Leaving Salina, thankfully few ferries turn west for the more distant tiny islands of Filicudi and Alicudi. Their remoteness has been their salvation.

Whale-shaped Filicudi is the nearer, and larger, of the two – a 9.8km² (3.8sq.mile) isle fashioned by man into terraced tiers and bound by ancient footpaths. But the islanders craved a road and so a short one cleaves through the heathers to link east with west. Filicudi's highest point, the 773m (2576ft) Fossa Felci is not only cloaked with the bracken that gave it its name, but with maquis and chestnut stands. Cape Graziano, the site of a Bronze Age village, lies atop the 'whale's tail'. It is an uphill scramble to the plateau where little but lichen-covered stones remain of the 25 huts, for the more important items are now housed in the Archaeological Museum. But the panorama justifies the exertion. At 5,2km²

(3sq.miles), cone-shaped Alicudi is the second smallest island in the group. It used to be known as Ericusa after the erica that swathes the soil. It is breathtaking: small, simple but very beautiful. An old and steep pathway climbs from Alicudi Port and tracks the contours leading to the church of San Bartolo. Transport is four-legged: donkeys labour under their miscellaneous loads descending stepped paths while the locals tend to their vineyards and the ubiquitous caper. With its garlic, chilli, tomatoes, pasta and fish or seafood, Aeolian cuisine is rustic but healthy.

Alicudi's fortunes have improved in the last couple of decades for a number of visitors have adopted the island, eschewing mainland Italy for the simple pleasures of living without supermarkets, cinemas and motorized transport. They have freshened up the pastel-coloured homes and helped swell the dwindling population. They also helped bring electricity to Alicudi. With remarkable foresight, the supply was laid below ground.

Skirting Salina, the ferry travels some 80km (50 miles) and docks at San Pietro, the only village on Panarea. This is the smallest isle, a mere 3.2km² (2sq.mile) loaf of land rising to the 421m (1400ft) peak of Monte del Corvo, and falling vertically into the sea on the west. But small does not mean insignificant; fashionably wealthy visitors have also discovered the rustic charms of Panarea, doubling its population of 276 during the summer and nudging hotel and restaurant bills skyward. But it is still worth every minute.

Like Alicudi and Salina, the architecture is solidly simple but softened with bowers of bougainvillea, myriad flower pots, steps and seductive arches rarely in need of a coat of paint. As in Alicudi, Bronze Age dwellers settled here and a 30-minute stroll leads to the excavated village of round huts at Cape Milazzese. Even if your archaeological interest is limited, you'll still appreciate the setting.

Panarea's coast lends itself to marine exploration – and sleek yachts abound in summer. Thought to be the remains of a submerged volcano, it is ringed by islets and sheltered coves where the turquoise waters tempt you to take the plunge.

And lastly to smoking Stromboli. Who can resist a good fireworks display? Stromboli is Europe's best provider of pyrotechnics. As you check into your hotel opposite the offshore lump of Strombolicchio, it can be mildly unnerving to learn that the last important eruption was in 2003 – the same year that Etna burst to smoke and spewed lava down its slopes towards Catania.

Many of the 550 islanders live on the north shore of this 12.6km² (4.9sq.mile) island, though some live in isolated Ginostra on the southwest, dwarfed by the highest of the multiple peaks, Serra dei Vancori. It peaks at 926m (3086ft) and some 200m (666ft) below the rim is the crater, but visitors are reassured that all volcanic activity takes place in a westerly direction, down the Sciara del Fuoco. Naturally, visitors are there to see the action and many take the easy option. Rather than gearing up at nighttime and hiking to the summit (a five-hour round trip), they can board a boat bound for the western side of the isle.

Of course, there is no guarantee of activity, however, and the only evidence of its violence that you may see may be little more than a reddish glow and rumbles and dull thuds that are felt, rather than heard. Like all natural phenomena, nothing is programmed but the boatman may promise your next trip will be more than just dud fireworks, and like a moth to a lamp, you probably will make another trip. For within this realm of wind, fire, earth and water, home to a proud and stoic people, there is more, much more to discover.

Above *Rows of colourful fishing boats bob on the water at the small harbour at Lipari.*

Opposite *As the sun sets, the view from Panarea island across the calm sea to the nearby island of Bazziluzzo is one of utter tranquility.*

Corsica

WILLIAM GRAY

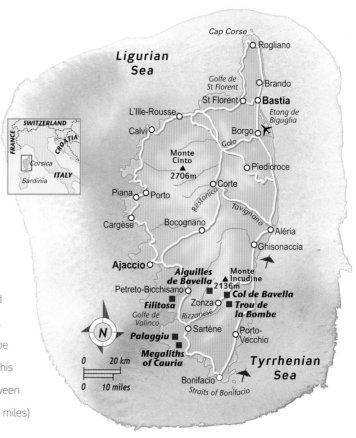

here can be few things more evocative of the Mediterranean than strolling through a swathe of Corsican maquis on a warm May afternoon. Herbs, gently crushed underfoot, infuse the air, while golden drifts of broom inflame entire hillsides. Rockrose, myrtle, rosemary and wild fennel add to the heady potpourri of aromatic shrubs and flowers that characterize this luxuriant landscape. Ambling through patchy groves of gnarled cork oaks, their trunks stripped of bark, you can hear the staccato hammer of woodpeckers and glimpse redstarts and wheatears chasing insects along ancient dry stone walls. With each step, grasshoppers and crickets flicker around your feet like green sparks, their ratchet mantras beating to the tranquil rhythm of the maquis.

Corsica seems a world away from the rampant resorts and crowded beaches that stereotype much of the Mediterranean. Although it still receives its fair share of summer holiday-makers, this enigmatic island remains one of the truly wild and unspoiled gems of the region. Located between the Tyrrhenian and Ligurian seas, Corsica's nearest mainland port is Piombino, about 100km (62 miles) away on the west coast of Italy. Politically, however, Corsica is part of France and has been for over two centuries. With an area of 8680km^2 (3350sq.miles) it is less than half the size of its southerly neighbour, Sardinia – a short ferry ride across the wind-swept Straits of Bonifacio.

Mysterious standing stones and other Neolithic remains provide tantalizing evidence that humans settled Corsica at least 6000 years ago. From Greek colonists and Roman conquerors to Genoese rulers, and a brief period of independence, the island has garnered a rich historical legacy. That's not to say, however, that Corsica has been tamed. This is an island of contrasts, an intriguing kaleidoscope of busy ports and impenetrable pine forests, ancient citadels and plummeting sea cliffs.

At the heart of Corsica, mountains rear above juniper scrub and grassy pastures, their flanks riven by deep gorges in which snowmelt froths and cascades. The tallest peak is Monte Cinto. At 2706m (8878ft) it is one of the highlights of the famous GR20 (*Grande Randonnée* 20) – a spectacular hiking trail that straddles 140km (87 miles) of Corsica's rugged interior.

Although more heavily populated, the coastline is no less impressive. Along its 1000km (620-mile) length there is a procession of granite headlands, white limestone cliffs and sandy bays.

Nowhere is Corsica's extraordinary diversity of landscape and vivid history more apparent or accessible than in the island's south. Teetering on a wave-scoured promontory near the southernmost tip of Corsica is the dramatic fortified city of Bonifacio. Approaching the medieval settlement by road, the sheer rock faces of the Bastion de l'Étendard rear above a marina packed with gleaming yachts and launches, and lined with outdoor restaurants – a far cry from the ninth and 10th centuries when the town thrived on fishing and piracy. Named for the Marquis of Tuscany, Bonifacio was partly ruled by Pisa before becoming a Genoese republic in 1195. Prosperous times ensued with the construction of massive walls and the Ste-Marie-Majeure – the fine cathedral that dominates Bonifacio's *haute ville* (upper town).

A road winds up to this lofty warren of narrow streets and crowded houses, but not only are the stairs – known as Montée Rastello – more satisfying, but they also help you to better appreciate Bonifacio's supremely strategic position. Invading armies would have had a tough time attempting to storm the town, while the harbour in the inlet below appears practically unassailable. However, it is only when you burrow through the *haute ville* and emerge on the seaward side of the promontory, which is 350m (1150ft) wide, that you're struck by Bonifacio's *pièce de résistance*:

Right *The extravagant outermost houses in Bonifacio's* haute ville *teeter on the edge of precipitous limestone sea cliffs.*

Opposite *Built in the 16th century to house powerful artillery, the massive Bastion de l'Etenard towers over the marina at Bonifacio.*

limestone cliffs that plunge 60m (200ft) into the rock-strewn carnage of Corsica's most stunning coastline.

The constant gnawing of wind and sea, coupled with Bonifacio's chronic shortage of space, have conspired to leave the outermost buildings perched on the very brink of the cliffs. For the best views, though, you need to return to the marina where local boat operators offer trips along the coast.

From sea level, Bonifacio looms precariously overhead, its buildings sprouting above the striated cliffs of limestone like clustered crystals. This audacious feat of engineering is embellished by the Escalier du Roi d'Aragon, a rock-hewn stairway that descends the most precipitous section of cliff – 187 steps from town to sea level.

Even without human presence, Bonifacio's coastline would still prove a crowd-puller. Numerous caves have been chiselled into the cliffs, while magnificent sea stacks, like the curiously named Grain de Sable (Grain of Sand), have been severed from the mainland. On an island otherwise dominated by igneous rocks, Bonifacio's chalky cliffs are something of an anomaly on Corsica. However, you need only travel

a short distance north before the road begins grappling with the granite mountains of the interior. At Zonza, a small town well known as a centre for hiking, climbing and rafting, the profile of the Aiguilles de Bavella stands proud above slopes of oak and pine forest. This imposing rampart of sawtooth peaks forms part of the Monte Incudine massif that rises to 2136m (7008ft).

Continuing along the D268 road north of Zonza, you enter the realm of large raptors, like the golden eagle and bearded vulture. Domestic goats graze along the precipitous road verges, but the high mountain regions are also home to the much scarcer mouflon – a wild goat species that was near extinction on Corsica before it was declared a protected species in 1956. Nowadays, there are around 600 of these sturdy, spiral-horned beasts on the island and it has become Corsica's symbol.

At the Col de Bavella, meadows smothered in thyme, alpine asphodel and the glorious orange-flowered martagon lily sprawl beneath weather-beaten Laricio pines – some of which are believed to have reached the venerable age of 800 years. Rarities such as the Corsican pinguicula, a dainty white or mauve flower that is just one of the island's endemic plants, can also be found here. Understandably, the Col de Bavella has become a magnet for walkers. The southernmost stages of the long-distance GR20 path traverse the area, but for those with less time or stamina several short walks are also available. One of the most interesting is the two-hour jaunt

to the Trou de la Bombe, a peculiar hole 9m (30ft) high, which has been eroded through a rock face. Found throughout Corsica, these so-called *tafoni* can also take the form of natural cavities. Curious as they may seem to modern day ramblers, *tafoni* once played an important role in the lives of early Corsicans, who used them as burial sites or simple shelters.

To the west of Bavella, just inland from the Golfe de Valinco, there is more palpable evidence of some of the island's earliest colonists. At Filitosa, in 1946, a remarkable discovery was made of a fortified settlement dating back to 1800BC. Ancient stone walls were painstakingly excavated, but nothing could have prepared archaeologists for the wealth of statue menhirs that the site has also yielded. Reaching up to twice the height of a man, these mysterious standing stones still display markings of weapons and faces – no doubt of the warriors whom the stones were honouring nearly 4000 years ago. The most famous is known simply as Filitosa V – a slab of granite etched with a long sword and sheathed dagger.

Filitosa is not the only place in southern Corsica to have shed light on the island's past. No less than 500 prehistoric sites have been identified on the plateau of Cauria, south of Filitosa. Renaggiu boasts Corsica's oldest artefacts, with menhirs dating from 4000BC. Nearby are Stantari's pink standing stones and the dolmen of Fontanaccia. However, even these finds pale beside the incredible 'stone forest' of Palaggiu,

where some 258 menhirs form one of the world's most important alignments of these mesmerizing monuments.

The long history of Corsica can be traced at the Musée de Préhistoire Corse et d'Archéologie in Sartène, midway between Filitosa and Cauria. This atmospheric hilltop town also warrants a visit in its own right. Perched on a hill above the valley of the Rizzanese River, Sartène resembles a stony house of cards, its terracotta-roofed buildings abutting each other with, it seems, barely a chink for an alleyway. But probing the town on foot soon leads you into a maze of narrow cobbled streets, hemmed in by mansions or less grand town houses, whose whitewashed plaster has begun to crack and flake.

Sartène is the setting for one of the oldest religious ceremonies on Corsica. Each Good Friday evening, the Catenacciu Procession leaves the Baroque church of Ste-Marie to re-enact Christ's crucifixion walk to Golgotha. Black-robed figures carry the statue of the Dead Christ while onlookers chant 'Perdonu miu Diu' (Forgive me Lord). The solemn parade is led by the Catenacciu, or 'Great Penitent' – a hooded figure clad in chains, who bears the Cross through Sartène's streets.

The vast majority of Corsicans are Catholic. Commemoration of Holy Week, the island's most important annual event, takes place not only in Sartène but also in towns and cities throughout Corsica. In the 15th-century Genoese citadels of Bastia and Calvi in northern Corsica, grand cathedrals play a central role during Easter and other religious celebrations when revered icons, like Bastia's Christ des Miracles – the protector of fishermen – are paraded around town.

A sense of pride and identity are mainstays of Corsican culture. The age-old custom of vendettas, in which families feuded over anything from land to women, may be a thing of the past, but Corsica's language (Corsu) remains entrenched in everyday life. Closer to Italian than French, Corsu derived from Latin, but evolved through centuries of Tuscan, Pisan and Genoan rule into something quite endemic. Despite the fact that France annexed the island in 1769, road signs are still written in Corsican and French. However, if there is one thing guaranteed to stir local pride, particularly in Ajaccio, it is the mere mention of Napoleon Bonaparte. Born here on 15 August 1769, the man destined to become emperor of France is still venerated in Corsica's largest city.

At the epicentre of Corsican culture is the city Corte – unique on the island in that it is located not on the coast but high in the mountains. Like the cliff-top city of Bonifacio in the south, Corte commands a majestic setting – its 13th-century Citadelle perched on a rocky outcrop overlooking the Restonica and Tavignano valleys. It was here, in 1735, that the constitution for an independent state was drafted in response to new taxes imposed by the Genoese rulers six years earlier. The struggle for autonomy continued until 1755, when Pascal Paoli finally succeeded in

Above *Tinted pink at sunset, the megalithic menhirs at Stantari bear testament to Corsica's rich archaeological legacy.*
Opposite *The needlike peaks of the Aiguilles de Bavella are a popular challenge for hikers and rock climbers.*

establishing the framework that would lead to 14 years of independence. On 8 May 1769, however, nationalist troops were defeated by the French at the battle of Ponte-Novo. Paoli's dream to purge Corsica of foreign dominion was over and French rule began.

Far from being forgotten, though, Paoli's legacy lives on today in the University of Corsica, which he founded in Corte. Snug behind austere bastions of stone, the university is just one of the buildings protected within the Citadelle. There is also a castle dating from 1419, and an anthropological museum housed in barracks that were once used by the Foreign Legion. Protruding from the highest point of the bastions, a small platform known as the *Nid d'Aigle* (eagle's nest) offers sweeping views of the surrounding mountains; rocky crags rising above hidden gorges, and distant ridges concealing remote valleys. Standing there, gazing across the wild, spirited heart of Corsica, it is hard to imagine that this is an island rising from one of the world's best-known and most populated seas. From the dappled shade of its traditional cork oak forests to the rarely trodden trails of its mountain passes, Corsica still manages to inspire a sense of wonder and exploration in the midst of the crowded Mediterranean.

Korcula

ROBIN McKELVIE

As if giving birth to the most famous explorer the world has ever known was not enough, the Croatian island of Korcula also boasts a string of attractions that stir up the obvious question of why Marco Polo ever felt the need to go anywhere else? Fringed by the rugged limestone mountains of the Croatian littoral, blessed with some of the cleanest seas in Europe and reclining in a climate that brings the best out of both its people and its famous wine grapes, Korcula may just be the most appealing of all the Croatian islands and that is saying something, as there are 1185 to choose from.

Korcula hangs on the very edge of the Peljesac Peninsula roughly halfway down the sinuous Croatian coastline in the Dalmatia region, with the mainland and the former Yugoslav republic of Bosnia to the north and the Adriatic Sea and Italy stretching away to the south. The island is accessible by ferry

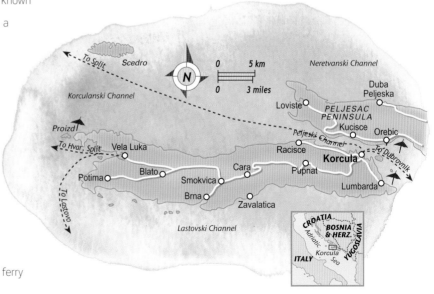

from the mainland resort of Orebic just across the narrow Peljeski Channel and from the Croatian cities of Dubrovnik or Split, with the arrival by ferry a dramatic one amid the spires and orange roof tiles of Korcula Town.

The willowy island, much of which is lavishly painted in a cloak of pine trees and green scrub, stretching for 47km (29 miles) from east to west, is never more than 7km (4.5 miles) in width. Its indented coastline wraps around numerous bays, coves and inlets, with a sprinkling of neighbouring islands temptingly just offshore.

Korcula was first settled by the Greeks who dubbed it 'Black Corfu', given its mass of woodland, but it was the Venetians who had the greatest impact on Korcula, arriving in the 10th century and lingering on for another 800 years — they left an impressive architectural legacy. By the 20th century, Korcula had lost its strategic importance and settled into a comfortable middle age, but today the island is experiencing something of a renaissance as Croatia emerges as one of Europe's rising tourist stars.

These days Marco Polo is fast becoming Korcula's Loch Ness Monster. In a similar way that the elusive monster propels tourism at the Scottish loch, Korcula's claim to being the birthplace of the legendary explorer Marco Polo has helped boost visitor numbers in recent years. Whether Polo, whom Venice and Genoa both also claim as their own, was in fact born on this Dalmatian island may never be known, but the matter is somewhat irrelevant considering the charm of even a 'Marco Polo-less' Korcula.

Korcula Town itself is the island's main draw, a historic oasis that vies with Dubrovnik and Kotor for the accolade of the most attractive town on the Adriatic coast. This dizzying chocolate-box beauty of old stone houses, crumbling churches and cobbled streets spreads out across its own peninsula. Exploring is easy, with a thoroughfare running right through the heart of the old core and a waterside boulevard circling the peninsula. All around are sweeping views of the mainland mountains and the Peljeski Channel.

Right *The main spire and façade of St Mark's Cathedral display a rich mix of architectural styles, making this building a landmark in Korcula Town.*

Opposite *The houses of Korcula's Old Town almost completely surround the harbour; the orange-tiled roofs are typical of houses on the island.*

Korcula Town's most dramatic building is St Mark's Cathedral. This triple-naved basilica's interior impresses with a cocktail of architectural styles; gothic and renaissance take centre stage. There is a figure of a woman in the façade surrounded by a gaggle of monsters, but no one really knows exactly who she is, though there have been suggestions that she may have been the wife of the Roman Emperor Diocletian, a man with a well-documented penchant for throwing Christians to the lions.

The cathedral is also home to an Annunciation by celebrated Italian artist Tintoretto, who spent time in Korcula as a student. The altarpiece on the wall of the apse carries depictions of the saints Bartholomew, Jerome and Mark, the patron saints of Korcula, who were said to have helped repel the Ottomans when they besieged the town on the way north to the Battle of Lepanto in the 16th century. The pikes and other weapons are relics of the struggle against the Ottomans.

Art lovers should also head next door from the cathedral to the Bishop's Treasury, which crams a surprising amount of works by an eclectic array of artists into its small confines. The building itself was restored in the 17th century with the addition of a hanging garden. Spread across seven small halls is the collection, with

Above *The rolling vineyards of Korcula's interior, where the island's famous wine grapes are harvested; visitors can also look out for the wine houses, where they can sample the local wine.*

Opposite *Korcula's Old Town is completely surrounded by sturdy, white stone walls overlooking the ocean, and looking back towards mainland Croatia.*

works by Bassano, Carpaccio and various Croatian luminaries. Also part of the collection are gold, silver and porcelain artefacts, medieval pottery and, somewhat bizarrely, a figure of Mary Queen of Scots.

Given the level of local pride, it is impossible to resist a visit to the Marco Polo House, where the explorer was said to have been born in 1254. It is clear that Polo spent at least some time in Korcula, so the legend may well be true. His role as the world's first travel writer is, however, more dubious as there have been suggestions that he never even visited China, and made up most of his stories from reports and other tall tales. There is little to actually see inside the house, but the walk to the top floor is well worth it for the sweeping vista of terracotta-tiled roofs, clear blue sea and pine-clad hills.

If you can tear yourself away from Korcula Town, and most people do not find it easy, there is the rest of the island to explore. The landscape is largely made up of vineyards and forests, a perfect venue for taking a tour by bicycle or renting a car, although for those short on time the Skoji islands can be reached easily by boat from Korcula Town. With your own wheels you can just cruise around, stopping off at a small cove or ramble of shingle beach that appeals. Also look out for the small wine houses where you can sample the local wines and buy a bottle or two at knockdown prices.

Outside Korcula Town the only other villages really worth visiting are Lumbarda and Blato, which both have nearby beaches for those looking to savour the languorous Mediterranean climate. One of Korcula's greatest pleasures is just stumbling upon a restaurant, preferably with an outdoor terrace, and lazing away an

afternoon. Most specialize in fresh Adriatic seafood such as squid, mussels and sea bass, washed down, of course, with a glass or two of the wine that the island produces in such abundance.

Korcula is also home to perhaps the most famous folk dance in all of Croatia – the Moreka – and Korcula Town is 'the' place to experience this traditional dance. Local men troop through town in summer in their elegant bright red and deep black costumes as they head for the open-air arena. The dance has its origins deep in the 15th century and basically recounts the tale of two kings, the white king who is somewhat confusingly kitted out in red and the black king who sticks to his own colour. Unsurprisingly, a fair maiden is involved and the two battle over her affections as she struggles to escape the black king and realize her true love.

A dozen supporters of both kings draw their swords and dance a colourful routine of seven fights, which make up the main body of a performance that is enhanced by the setting sun as a backdrop. You half expect Marco Polo to breeze in, and one night a year he actually does, when in reality a local dressed as the great explorer drifts ashore aboard an old sailing ship to a rapturous welcome from the island's inhabitants.

Perhaps Polo's greatest tribute to the island was that the man who perhaps had seen more of the world than anyone before, chose to return from his wanderings to his native Korcula.

Above right *Marco Polo makes a triumphant return to his native Korcula as part of Marco Polo Day.*

Right *Fresh produce, used in the preparation of a range of tantalizing local dishes to tempt the palate, bring a riot of colour to Korcula's market.*

Opposite *At night, Korcula's Old Town becomes very quiet and there is no sign of tourists or residents roaming the streets.*

Malta

BRIAN RICHARDS

*M*alta and its small 'sisters', Gozo and Comino, are rocky limestone outcrops rising from the Mediterranean, cultural crossroads between Europe and Africa, with a long and eventful history dating back 6500 years. The past is evident in the ancient temples, palaces, churches and fortifications dotted about the islands; the present and future are wrapped up in the independent republic's recent political accession to the European Union.

'Malta' applies to both the country and the largest of the Maltese islands, which lies 93km (58 miles) south of Sicily and 288km (180 miles) east of Tunisia. Malta has a total area of 246km² (95sq.miles) and the smaller Gozo has an area of 67km² (26sq.miles), and an even tinier Comino is just 2.7km² (1sq.mile). The islands vary widely in appearance. Malta slopes gently from 243m (800ft) cliffs in the south to the heavily populated northern shore,

its rugged terrain often semi-arid in appearance, bearing few of the trees that once covered the island. Gozo, on the other hand, is far greener and more fertile, due to the land's underlying blue clay that effectively conserves rainwater. Between them, in the middle of the Comino Channel, sits barren Comino.

On Malta and Gozo, crops grow in a patchwork of tiny fields bound by rough limestone walls. Despite the lack of rain for much of the year, these small enclosures of red-brown soil yield a wide variety of produce – among them are tomatoes, capers and melons. Grapes are used in local wine production and there are small plantations of olives, carobs and figs.

Although the islands have sandy beaches, there are only a few and you have to know where they are. Most are located in the northern part of Malta; Mellieha Bay is the largest, popular with windsurfers, while across a narrow neck of land are Golden Bay and Ghajn Tuffieha Bay – smaller bays, with rich golden-colour sand; there are a couple of small sandy beaches on Gozo. These stretches of coastline fill quickly to overload in summer, when the sun blazes from a clear blue sky for 12 hours a day, and temperatures rise up to 35°C (95°F). The Maltese islands boast Europe's best sunshine record, and the winter climate is good, too – days are mild with only the occasional burst of rain. While summer tourists crave Malta's sun, sea and sand, winter visitors are attracted to the island's history – most prominently, the proud legacy of the Knights of St John of Jerusalem who fought for Christendom.

Wherever you turn in the capital Valletta, and across the Grand Harbour in Vittoriosa, Senglea and Cospicua – three small towns collectively known as the 'Three Cities' – you are constantly aware of the Knights' influence on this island. A chivalric order that combined soldiering with nursing, the Knights showed up in 1530, having been handed Malta by Charles V, Holy Roman Emperor and King of Spain and Sicily. Most notably, under the guidance of Grand Master Jean Parisot de la Valette, the Knights created Valletta on a finger of land between the island's two great natural harbours.

With its streets conforming to a strict grid pattern, Valletta became Europe's first 'new town', laid out within massive defensive walls. Many splendid buildings of the Knights still remain – these include the mighty hospital, or Sacra Infirmeria; the Palace of the Grand Masters; and the fine auberges (headquarters) of the Knights.

Gaze from Valletta's ramparts across Grand Harbour and you can easily picture the scene as it was back in the late 16th century: the massive Fort St Angelo, the long harbour inlets filled with the Knights' galleys, and the brand new capital rising

behind you on Scibberas hill. Valletta was built following the bloody eviction of the Turks in the Great Siege of 1565 to replace Mdina as Malta's capital. Now free of traffic, Mdina is a living museum that's known as the 'Silent City'; it covers just 4ha (10 acres) and within its walls are a cathedral, palaces, churches, convents, homes of the Maltese nobility and a small hotel.

Right *Malta's capital Valletta was founded by the Knights of St John after the Great Siege in 1566. The fortress city was completed in just 15 years.*

Opposite *Defended by the 16th-century Fort St Angelo, Grand Harbour is widely viewed as the world's greatest natural harbour.*

The islands that attracted the warlike attention of Süleyman the Magnificent and his Turkish raiders had 2500 years earlier provided a base for Phoenician traders. They carved the eye of Osiris on the prow of their boats to ward off evil spirits, a practice continued today by Maltese fishermen, who steer their brightly coloured luzzu craft seaward in search of tuna, sword-fish, acciola, dentici (sea bream) and cerna (grouper).

The Phoenicians were followed by the Carthaginians, and today the Maltese people can trace their ancestory back to those early settlers. Likewise to the Romans – Malta was part of the Roman Empire for 800 years – the Byzantines, Arabs and Normans followed. Down the centuries, Malta has evolved as a cultural melting pot.

When St Paul was shipwrecked on Malta in AD60, he spread the seeds of Christianity on the island and as a result the Maltese people are devoutly Catholic. There is a church for every 1100 of Malta's 391,000 population, ranging in size from the mighty cathedrals of Valletta and Mdina to tiny roadside chapels. There are many small communities scattered about Malta and Gozo and each village is dominated by its church – giant edifices built of yellow limestone blocks and topped by dark red domes that soar majestically towards the heavens. One of the two towers bears a ticking clock and the other a painted clock face – to confuse the devil, it is said.

For the Maltese, Easter has special significance, with lengthy Good Friday processions in which life-size wooden tableaux depicting the Passion and death of Christ are carried through the streets. The parades on Easter Sunday are much more upbeat, with church bells ringing out as statues of the risen Christ are car-ried through towns and villages.

As a nation, Malta is heavily into parades and pro-cessions, and between April and September each parish holds its *festa* to celebrate the local patron saint's day. Local organizations take part and everyone falls in behind the local brass band along streets filled with flags and bunting. Throughout the *festa* period the parish church is decked out with hundreds of light bulbs,

Above *Mattia Preti created the beautiful scenes on the vault of St John's Cathedral. He painted directly on stone, having first prepared it with oil.*

Right *The dome of Mosta Parish Church, a 19th-century church styled on Rome's Pantheon, rises above Mosta beyond fields of spring flowers.*

Opposite *High-prowed luzzu fishing boats, their design unaltered in centuries, are a colourful feature of Marsaxlokk fishing village.*

stalls sell sweet confectionery and everyone has a fantastic time while the band plays on. The celebrations wind up with a lavish firework display for which the parishioners have raised money throughout the year.

It was the fun-loving Knights who first used religion as a reason for celebration when they introduced Malta's pre-Lent Carnival back in the 16th century. The islanders have keenly kept the tradition going, and today everyone joins in the fun with decorated floats, fancy dress parades, music and dancing – and yet more fireworks.

Malta's passion for festivals extends further, to take in all kinds of music, from rock and jazz to choral; food and drink; and heritage in the Historic Cities Festival held in the Three Cities each October, where folklore and pageantry rule the day.

On the question of food, while restaurant fare is broadly a mix of British – the legacy of 150 years of British rule that ended in 1964 – and Mediterranean, Malta has some fine traditional recipes of its own. Start with aljotta, a fish soup with tomatoes and garlic, or minestra, a heavier soup with pasta and vegetables, and follow with bragoli – thin slices of beef rolled around minced ham and pork, bacon, egg and

peas – or stewed octopus in a sauce of onions, olives, tomatoes and capers. For a lighter appetite, the Maltese have their own version of ravioli, filled with ricotta cheese rather than meat. For the ravenously hungry, there's always timpana – macaroni that's baked golden brown with a heavyweight mix of minced beef and pork, chicken liver, bacon, eggs and cheese.

Maltese wine is produced from grapes imported from Sicily and northern Italy, though some are grown locally. The quality of Maltese wine has improved in recent years, and among the best bottles to be had are the local Merlot and Pinot Grigio.

Well over a million people travel to Malta on holiday each year to soak up its sunshine, feast on its food and immerse themselves in its culture. It's little wonder that tourism has grown to become the country's major industry.

Santorini

ROBIN GAULDIE

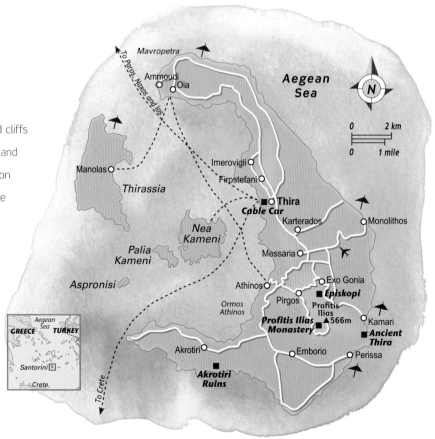

*A*wesome in their apocalyptic grandeur, Santorini's multicoloured cliffs rise from their sea-filled caldera in strata of black, red, grey and creamy white pumice, relics of a millennia-old cultural extinction event that shook the ancient world of the eastern Mediterranean and the Middle East to its foundations.

The cliffs rise from an undersea crater more than 100m (328ft) deep and 3km (1.86 miles) across. This crescent of pumice, ash and metamorphic marble is all that remains of a larger island, vapourized in 1750BC in a volcanic explosion that wrecked Europe's first civilization. Vulcanologists estimate that the Thira explosion was vastly more powerful than the most powerful volcanic blast of modern times, the Krakatoa (or Krakatau) eruption of the late 19th century.

The event unleashed tsunamis and tremors that wrecked the palaces and cities of Minoan Crete and lashed the coasts of Egypt and Asia Minor.

Clouding the skies with ash and dust, it may have set off a 'nuclear winter' that is reflected in the myths of flood and plague, common to the legends of Egypt, Sumer and the Bible's Old Testament, which are traced to around the time of the eruption.

Some scholars have argued, convincingly, that the island is also the original Atlantis, which was described by the ancient philosopher Plato as a lost civilization that long pre-dated the world of the Greek city-states.

Atlantis, Plato recorded, encompassed a huge lagoon, surrounded by cliffs and reached by a narrow sea-channel – a description that could be taken to match Santorini and its deep caldera quite well.

This stark landscape can seem a little ghostly at times, especially in winter when the island is bereft of visitors – it's not entirely surprising that Santorini is notoriously the abode of the *vrokolakas*. This Greek version of the vampire bears no resemblance to the shape-shifting bloodsucker of Transylvanian legend; rather a disembodied spirit that wails at night, foretelling death or calamity – it seems rather similar to the banshee of Irish folklore.

Lying six to eight hours of sailing southeast of Athens and around 80km (50 miles) north of the great island of Crete, Santorini is the southernmost of the Cyclades group in Greece's Aegean Sea. Legend has it that Santorini's first inhabitants were the Pelasgians, who named their island 'Kallisti' (the most beautiful). Two centuries after the great volcanic eruption, it was resettled by Spartans from the southern mainland, who then renamed it Thira, after their King Thiras. That name stuck until the Christian era, when it was again renamed in honour of St Irene of Thessaloniki, who was martyred in 304. In later centuries, it became Santorini.

The island forms a long, rugged crescent around 32km (20 miles) from its northern point to its southern tip, and is no more than 2km (1.24 miles) wide. Divided from east to west by a steep mountain ridge that rises to 566m (1857ft) at its highest point, high cliffs line the inner, western coast and a landscape of terrace fields slopes gently to the long curving charcoal-grey volcanic sand beaches of the east coast.

Right *The beautiful blue-domed churches, like these overlooking the sea at Oia, are typical on the island of Santorini.*

Opposite *Majestic cruise ships often anchor below Thira and visitors to the island ride on a mule from the quay to this main village.*

These ashy slopes, which are almost treeless, except for a few outcrops of figs and prickly pear, and trickles of pink flowering oleander look rather unpromising. However, the soil is fertile and produces rich harvests of plum tomatoes, which are among the island's main cash crops. The rich soil and scorching summer sun – temperatures can rise to 40°C (104° F) in July and August – produce small, intensely sweet muscat grapes which are used to make Vin Santo, a dessert wine. In the 18th and 19th centuries, it was prized by the nobility of Czarist Russia, leading to a thriving wine trade between Santorini and Odessa on the Black Sea. These days, sticky sweet wines are out of fashion. Vin Santo is still made, but Santorini has moved with the times and winemakers, like the Boutari Company, now use the grapes to make a range of drier, more sophisticated vintages as well as sweet dessert wines.

Thira, the main village, is 275m (902ft) above sea level and can be reached by a zigzag donkey stairway with 566 steps, or by cable car. A clutter of white and pastel-pink buildings spills over the cliff-edge and down towards the sea, and a cobbled pathway leads to a small quay where excursion boats and tenders from the cruise ships dock. It's a steep hike from sea level to the village, and for decades muleteers earned a good living transporting less energetic visitors; the construction of a cable car link in the late 1980s caused much indignation, demonstrations and even threats of sabotage from the mule-owners, who saw it as a threat to their living. An eventual compromise was reached and, happily for the muleteers, there are

still plenty of people who would rather entrust themselves to traditional transport than to vertigo-inducing modern technology.

Tourism — in the shape of the cruise industry — had an early impact on Thira. The village is still one of the prettiest in the Aegean Sea, a typically Cycladic maze of whitewashed walls and arches interspersed with a scattering of medieval Venetian mansions, dating from the years when the Sanudo Dukes of Naxos ruled the island on behalf of the Venetian Republic. However, virtually every building is dedicated to parting visitors from their money. Bars and restaurants, souvenir shops, travel agencies, boutiques and jewellers abound in this village.

North of the historic centre, Thira has spread along the crater's edge to merge with the outlying villages of Firostefani and Imerovigli in a strip of pretty villas,

taverna restaurants, which all share the same stunning views, and clusters of charming boutique hotels — some of which have been converted from the barrel-roofed cave-houses called *skafta* that are typical of the island. Because Santorini is mainly composed of volcanic ash and soft pumice, villagers adapted to their island's peculiar geology by tunnelling homes, granaries and donkey stables into the soft volcanic tuff.

Beyond Firostefani, the cliff-edge becomes less cluttered and a walker's path leads all the way to Oia, on the very northern tip of the island. In 1956, this spectacularly located village was virtually destroyed by the tremors that accompanied a minor eruption of the still active Thira volcano — part of a wider series of quakes that three years earlier shook many of the Greek islands, including Kefalonia and Zakynthos in the Ionian group, and tiny Agios Efstratios in the northeast Aegean. The villagers were evacuated and re-housed elsewhere by the government and Oia lay crumbling for more than 30 years, until Greece's entry to the European Community — now called the European Union — gave access to funds for reconstruction. Today, it's hard to believe that this chic and colourful community of desirable Santorini's east coast bore the full impact of the tourism invasion of the 1980s; and Kamari, a sprawling but low-rise resort of small hotels and self-catering apartments built to meet the needs of package holiday-makers, is the result. Happily flowering bougainvillea, morning glories and tamarisk trees have softened its edges.

Kamari's sweep of charcoal sand is brought to an abrupt halt by the hulking mass of Profitis Ilias, the mountain ridge that cuts the island almost in two. Close to its highest point is the monastery of Profitis Ilias, which is just one of many such monasteries and churches throughout the Greek islands dedicated to the Prophet Elijah. Almost always these are set on, or close to, each island's highest summit in commemoration of the Old Testament prophet's ascent to Heaven in a fiery chariot; it doesn't take much imagination to guess that these Christian places of worship are sited on the foundations of temples to a much more ancient deity: Helios, driver of the God Apollo's sun-chariot. In Greek, the two names sound almost identical, and it seems likely that, as the old Olympian pantheon of the Hellenic world succumbed to Christianity in the fourth and fifth centuries AD, these older places of worship simply underwent a change of management.

Close to the monastery are the remnants of Ancient Thira — a few scattered walls and scraps of mosaic floor are all that remain, but the view from here is magnificent, with the southern half of the island spread out below, the long sweep of coast vanishing into the blue misty distance and, on a clear spring day, the rocky crag of Santorini's eastern neighbour, Anafi, jutting on the eastern horizon.

The steep ridge of Profitis Ilias divides the northern part of the island from the much less visited southern part and, on its shoulders, the sleepy hill village of Pirgos looks out over miles of vineyards and tomato fields. Here, apart from a few cognoscenti staying at the stylish Zannos Melathron hotel — once the mansion of the island's wealthiest wine-exporting dynasty – there are few visitors and life is less dependent on tourism: the donkeys in the narrow lanes, and their sombrero-wearing owners, are still working the land, not hauling cruise passengers for a living.

From the tumbledown ramparts of the little Venetian fortress tower that once crowned the village, you can look south through the blue summer haze to Akrotiri, the southern cape of Santorini. Here, in 1974, Greek archaeologists, led by Professor Spyridon Marinatos, unearthed evidence of one of the ancient world's most dazzling civilizations. Tragically, a wall collapsed on Marinatos.

At first, archaeologists theorized that the site at Akrotiri showed that Thira must have been an outpost of the Minoan empire on Crete, part of the same heritage as the ruins of Knossos, Festos, Malia and Zakros. But an even more fascinating hypothesis has emerged: perhaps Thira, before its destruction, was the cradle of that first European civilization, and the palace cities of Crete were its colonies.

The apocalypse that swallowed the island and its people some 3750 years ago means this can only be conjecture, but a visit to Akrotiri is mandatory; archaeologists are still unearthing mosaics and the walls of houses from the vanished civilization.

Tantalizingly close to Santorini, the islands of Aspronisi (white island) and Thirassia, like their larger neighbour, rise sharply from the caldera. Aspronisi is uninhabited, but Thirassia's sea-cliffs are crowned with a scattering of small white houses. Unlike Santorini, it has hardly been touched by tourism, and most of its tiny population make their living from fishing. It's easy enough to visit Thirassia, and it's well worth it, if only for the amazing view of Santorini from the west. En route, the day-trip caiques which ply between the two islands, usually anchor next to the Kameni (burnt) islands, a group of tiny skerries pushed up from the seabed by vulcanism as recently as the 1950s. A whiff of sulphur hangs over their black boulders, and those bold enough to plunge overboard will find the sea almost uncomfortably warm because of the submarine hot springs that emerge from the undersea slopes of the islands. It's a slightly unnerving reminder that Poseidon, ancient god of earthquakes and the sea, is only slumbering, and that Santorini's existence is still precarious.

Above right *The tiny fishing harbour of Ammoudi, northwest of Oia, has some fine old-fashioned fish tavernas.*

Right *Mules carry visitors up the hundreds of steps that connect clifftop Thira with the harbour.*

Opposite *Watch as the sun sets over the caldera, with Nea Kameni in the foreground and Thirassia on the horizon.*

Rhodes

ROBIN GAULDIE

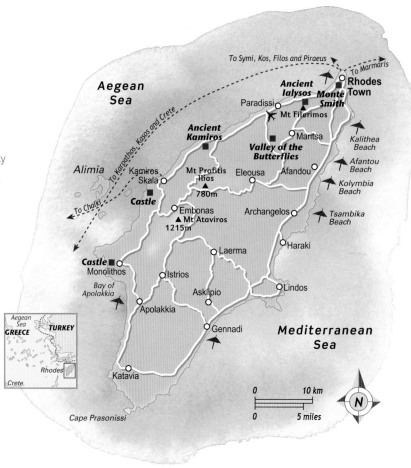

Rhodes is Greece in microcosm. Packed into an island of only 1398km² (540sq.miles) are relics of the heyday of the Classical/Greek world, the Roman and Byzantine empires, the Frankish interregnum of the Knights Hospitallers, the long oppression of the Ottoman Empire and the brief, grandiose decades of Italy's Aegean mini-empire.

Of all the major Greek islands, Rhodes lies furthest from mainland Greece – it is a mere 16km (10 miles) from the Turkish mainland. Rhodes is the fourth largest of Greece's islands, but is the biggest and most important of the Dodecanese group (meaning 'twelve islands', although the chain embraces several more), with a length of 84km (52 miles) and a maximum width of 35km (22 miles). Its coastline is 220km (137 miles) long, and with some of Greece's best beaches and up to 300 sunny days a year, it is not surprising that the island's holiday resorts are some of the busiest in Greece.

A hilly hinterland is dominated by two massifs: the 1215m (3986ft) Mt Ataviros and the 780m (2625ft) Profitis Ilias, which form a rocky backbone. Beneath these summits, rolling hills, small fields and goat pastures enclosed within a honeycomb of dry stone walls and fertile farmland are interspersed with patches of scrubland typical of the eastern Mediterranean. In summer, the dry hillsides appear barren, but in the island's brief but colourful spring, every field and patch of wasteland blazes with yellow and scarlet poppies, crown daisies, turban buttercups and blue anchusa. When the autumn rains come in late October, there is a second spring, when pink and mauve cyclamens, colchicums, narcissus, and yellow and purple crocuses and fritillaries bloom in fields and woodland.

The island's history, through more than two millennia, has been intimately tied up with that of Asia Minor as well as with the Hellenic world. In Classical times, the independent city-states Ialyssos, Lindos and Kamiros, aligned themselves some-times with the great Asian power of Persia, sometimes with the Greek hegemonies of Athens or Sparta.

After the division of Alexander the Great's short-lived empire, the island with-stood Demetrios Poliorketes (the Besieger), son of one of Alexander's more effective generals. Rhodes flourished as an outpost of Rome. Languishing under the decadent Byzantine Empire, Rhodes fell into the hands of rampaging Saracen corsairs, and enjoyed a late flowering as a bastion of militant Christendom against Islam in the hands of the piratical Knights of the Order of St John.

The Knights bought the island from the Genoese in 1309 and held it for almost three centuries, until they were finally evicted by the janissaries of Suleyman the Magnificent in 1522 after a six-month siege. The huge stone balls fired by Suleyman's can-non litter the dry moat that surrounds the fortified citadel of the Knights, and one can only marvel that the walls withstood them for so long.

So impressed was Suleyman with their defiant heroism that the Knights were allowed to sail free

from Rhodes with their colours flying – only to re-appear as a thorn in the Sultan's side after the Hapsburg emperor Charles V gave them Malta as a base of operation.

And it is the battlements of the Old Town that are Rhodes's most dramatic sight. This is no sterile monument, although it is listed as a UNESCO World Heritage site and gets its fair share of day-trippers from the purpose-built package holiday resorts that stretch either side of the old island capital. The Old Town is the world's best preserved, living medieval city and, after dark, when most of the tourists have returned to their cruise ships or holiday hotels, its narrow streets with their arched doorways and softly lit courtyards, where cobblers and carpenters still have their little workshops, are quiet and peaceful.

Within the walls, the stone-flagged Street of the Knights is lined with the arched stone gateways of the Inns which were the headquarters of each of the eight 'tongues' or chapters of the Order: Auvergne, France, Provence, Germany, England, Italy, Aragon and Castile. At its western end looms the Palace of the Grand Masters, a romantic confection of bastions and turrets surrounding an arcaded inner courtyard and a tall, square tower that dominates the old town.

Right   *The Palace of the Grand Masters is a lavishly restored masterpiece of medieval architecture.*
Opposite   *Medieval battlements, palm trees and the domes of former mosques and hammams (Turkish baths) add to Old Town's oriental atmosphere.*

The Palace, and the Street of the Knights, owe their suspiciously good state of repair to none other than Benito Mussolini, who decreed their repair and restoration in the 1930s to adorn Italy's miniature empire in the Dodecanese (gained by an opportunistic land-grab from the crumbling Ottoman Empire during the Balkan War of 1912 and ratified after World War I, when Italy picked the winning side). There are more relics of this era outside the medieval walls, where the Italians built a string of mock-oriental public buildings, including a charmingly eccentric produce market midway along the harbour front.

Close to the palace, on *Odos Sokratous* (Socrates Street) are two relics of the centuries of Turkish rule. The Suleyman Mosque, built in 1523 on the orders of Suleyman the Magnificent to celebrate his conquest of the island, is a striking, pink-stuccoed building crowned by a graceful dome. Like the nearby Mustafa Pasha Mosque, it is still used as a place of worship by the island's small community of Greek Muslims — one of only a handful of Muslim communities remaining in Greece.

Appropriately for Greece's sunniest island, Rhodes in ancient times was dedicated to the worship of the god Apollo, and when Poliorketes gave up his siege of the island the Rhodians sold off his abandoned siege engines and with the profits commissioned the island's greatest sculptor, Chares of Lindos, to build the greatest bronze statue the world had ever seen, dedicated to the junior god Helios, the driver of Apollo's sun-chariot. Sadly, nothing remains of this wonder of the ancient

world, which was toppled by an earthquake in 225BC and lay in ruins until AD653 when an enterprising trader bought the wreckage from the island's Saracen conquerors; it is said that it took 900 camels to haul the scrap metal to his ships.

There are more relics of the Knights at Lindos, where the crumbling walls of one of their castles stand on a clifftop, surrounding the tumbled columns of an even more ancient Hellenistic acropolis and looking out over a perfect crescent bay and one of the most photographed island villages in Greece.

Lindos is a cubist dream of cobbled lanes and whitewashed houses enlivened by explosions of scarlet bougainvillea and purple morning glories. Sadly, no village this pretty can hope to escape the clutches of tourism for long, and Lindos displays all the hallmarks of half a century of pandering to the holiday industry.

There is little left of the ancient city-state of Lindos apart from its clifftop acropolis, and not much more remains of the rival cities of Ialysos, on the slopes of Mt Filerimos, nor of Kamiros, where only foundations and a few column-drums remain to give a sense of its former importance. Somewhat more satisfying is Monte Smith (just outside Rhodes Town and named for an English admiral of the Napoleonic Wars, who established a naval lookout post here) where a few graceful white marble pillars mark the site of a Temple of Pythian Apollo and overlook an 800-seat third century Odeion (theatre) and stadium.

Rhodes is one of the few Greek islands that can be visited year round, boasting 300 days of sunshine annually. That said, January, February and March can be cool, wet and windy. Visit in April and May for spring flowers and fewer crowds, or in autumn (September and October) for warm days, warm seas and cooler evenings. Rhodes is a very popular package-holiday island and its beaches, restaurants and sights are very busy from mid June until the end of August.

Above right *The columns of a Hellenistic temple crown the Acropolis above Lindos, surrounded by the ramparts of a castle of the Knights.*

Right *St Paul's Bay is named after Paul The Apostle, who was shipwrecked at Lindos, and is now a major tourist destination.*

Opposite *Lindos's crescent of golden sand and clear water is the village's main attraction.*

Kefalonia

ROBIN GAULDIE

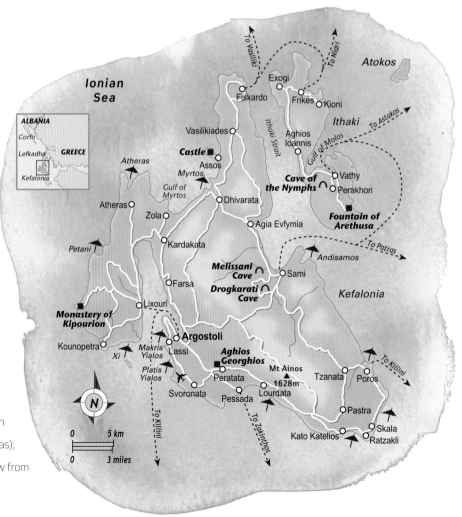

Hardly touched by tourism until its rise to fame as the setting for the film of Louis de Bernieres's novel *Captain Corelli's Mandolin*, Kefalonia is utterly different from the stereotype of a Greek island.

In place of barren brown hills grazed bare by herds of goats, this biggest and most prosperous of the Ionian islands is cloaked with lush forests and neat vineyards, and instead of whitewashed villages and blue-domed island chapels, its coasts are dotted with tidy, red-tiled fishing villages and its hillsides with the tottering walls of ruined Venetian citadels.

Kefalonia – also known as Cephallonia and Kefallinia – lies less than 20km (12 miles) from the western tip of the Peloponnese mainland. Within sight, to the north, is the smaller Ionian island of Lefkadha (Lefkada or Levkas); off to the south is Zakinthos – also known as Zante – and just a stone's throw from

Kefalonia's northern point is Ithaki (or Ithaca), home of the legendary Odysseus. Kefalonia is one of the largest islands in Greece, dwarfing its Ionian neighbours, with an area of 781km^2 (301sq.miles) and rising to one of the highest summits in the Greek islands, the 1628m (5341ft) Mt Ainos.

Thick forests of Kefalonian fir, *Abies cephalonica*, and plane trees cover the mountain's slopes, and its summit dominates a fertile central plain neatly planted with citrus trees, vines and ancient groves of gnarled olive trees which, in high summer, are shrill with the deafening sound of cicadas.

Kefalonia's summer heat is alleviated by occasional cooling breezes off the western sea, and its microclimate is a little less challenging than the blazing heat of the southern Greek isles. Autumn is warm and mellow; winter – from December to late March – is wet and windy, with a snowcapped Mt Ainos; and in April and May the fields, hills and roadsides are splashed with scarlet, blue and yellow wildflowers.

Rombola wine, nurtured by the summer sun and spring rains, is the pride of Kefalonia, and reckoned to stand head and shoulders above the sometimes impalatably harsh offerings of less-favoured isles.

The island's coasts are rugged, with white limestone cliffs plummeting into the most luminously blue seas in Greece.

Westward across the Ionian Sea, which merges with the Adriatic and the western Mediterranean, Italy is only a day's sailing away and at that close proximity has, sometimes tragically, shaped the island's history.

Like the rest of the Heptanissos (Seven Islands), as the Ionians are also known, Kefalonia fell nominally under Venetian control in the early 13th century, but in reality, it was ruled by a more or less piratical assortment of Italian nobles for most of the next two centuries. A brief occupation by the Ottoman Turks between 1479 and 1504 ended with a victory that left the island the sway of the Serene Republic for almost three centuries, until Venice was ousted in 1797 by revolutionary France. The French, in turn, were driven out by Russia and its ally Turkey; a short-lived United Septinsular Republic was terminated in 1809 with the arrival of the Royal Navy, and Britain set up a protectorate over all the Ionian islands that ended only in 1864, when they finally joined the young Kingdom of Greece.

The Italians returned in 1941, when Fascist Italy and its ally Nazi Germany invaded and occupied Greece, giving rise to the events fictionalized in de Bernieres's novel and film. In 1943, when Italy withdrew from the war, the Italian garrison (totalling 9000 men) repudiated its alliance with Germany and refused to surrender Kefalonia;

a nine-day battle followed. After the outgunned and outnumbered Italians surrendered, the Germans massacred all but 34 of the 5091 prisoners who had survived the fighting. They are commemorated at the Italian cemetery above the village of Aghios Theodori.

All this has left Kefalonia looking in some ways more Italian than Greek. There are scattered remnants of earlier Mycenean, Classical Greek and Roman settlements, but Kefalonia straddles a seismic fault line, and repeated earthquakes have

Right Kefalonia abounds in pretty little bays and coves such as this and while the island's main attraction is its beaches, these hideaways are also popular.

Opposite Fiskardo, near the northern tip of Kefalonia, is one of Greece's prettiest harbour villages and a popular port of call for yachts cruising these waters.

obscured much of its ancient history. The most recent of these, in 1953, accounts for the quaint mix of old Italianate houses and more modern buildings that dominate most of the island's villages and towns, including Sami and Lixouri – the main ferry ports – and Argostoli, the island capital which is a somewhat clumsy clutter of mostly modern buildings redeemed by a gorgeous setting on a calm double bay, reached by a remarkable causeway-bridge built by British army engineers.

For most visitors, Kefalonia's beaches are its main attraction, and the best ones – scattered along the south coast between Argostoli and Skala – each have their col-

lection of small hotels and guesthouses. The closest to the capital and its airport are Makris Yialos (Broad Beach) and Platis Yialos (Flat Beach), near Lassi, and they are understandably also the busiest and most developed. The sandy stretches between Kato Katelios and Ratzakli, close to Kefalonia's southeast tip, are reckoned the finest on the island. Sadly, the advent of tourism poses a threat to the endangered loggerhead turtles (*Caretta caretta*) which lay their eggs in the fine sand of this pretty bay; however, tourists as well as islanders have become more sensitive to the needs of egg-laying mother turtles and hatchlings, and conservation efforts continue.

turer from Sicily, who died here in an attempt to add Kefalonia to his little kingdom. It faces east, across a narrow strait, towards Kefalonia's little satellite, Ithaki, which is now a favourite holiday destination for yacht sailors and windsurfers. Fiskardo has a superb natural harbour at Vathy, on the Gulf of Molos, and it's easy to hop across on the ferry for a day's visit, or to rent a motorboat on the waterfront at Argostoli.

On the west coast, at the end of a challengingly steep zigzag road, the little fishing port of Assos contends with Fiskardo to be the prettiest island village. If anything, it's even quieter and more picturesque, with twin harbours overlooked by an impressive Venetian fortress.

Kefalonia's most impressive Venetian relic, however, is Aghios Georghios, the ruined medieval capital which stands above the more modern village of Peratata. Crowned by the colossal wreck of its castle, it gazes out over the fertile patchwork of the central plains from its hilltop.

But the sights that most visitors remember longest lie deep within Kefalonia's limestone rock, carved out by millennia of winter rain and melting snow. The island is honeycombed by deep grottoes. Most are off limits to casual visitors, but the Melissani Cave – where a deep, multihued pool some 0.2km (0.12 miles) long is lit by sunlight piercing openings where the cavern's roof caved in during the 1953 earthquake – can be explored by boat. It's an unforgettable climax to any visit to Captain Corelli's Island.

Above The glowing blue waters of the Melissani grotto, which can be explored by boat, are among the island's top sights.
Below right The serene village beach at Assos is overlooked by a row of quayside cafés and tavernas.
Opposite The white beach and turquoise waters of Myrtos are dazzling – but getting there calls for a good head for heights.

But Kefalonia's most spectacular beach is remarkably undeveloped – partly, perhaps, because it is at the end of a vertiginous zigzag road below the beetling limestone cliffs of the west coast. There are few hotels at Myrtos, but despite that it can be hard to find a place to lay your towel here in high season. Its blindingly white pebbles and sand, and vivid, clear blue sea attract visitors by the score.

If Kefalonia's larger towns seem a little less than picturesque, two attractive fishing villages set on the mountainous peninsula in the north of the island more than redress the balance.

Fiskardo, where a row of pastel-painted mansions stand behind a perfect, glassy clear natural harbour, takes its name from an 11th-century Norman adven-

Madeira

RODNEY BOLT

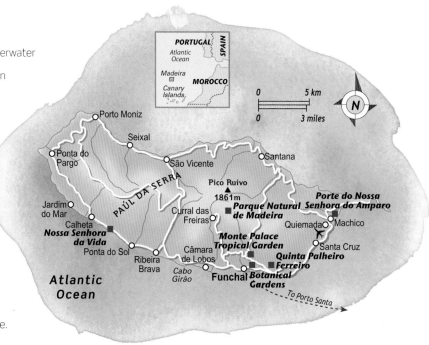

Madeira thrusts high out of the Atlantic, the very peak of an underwater mountain range that rises 5000m (16,405ft) above the ocean bed. It breaks surface suddenly, towering above the waves, shunning any idea of beaches, and snagging every passing cloud. Ancient mariners, noting the mists over its mountains, thought that Madeira was the Mouth of Hell. But its ample water supply, together with volcanic soil and a mild subtropical climate, add up to abundance. Orchids and tree ferns, lilies, bougainvillea and agapanthus, flowering trees and rampant creepers drape the island and lead to another moniker: the Isle of Flowers. The sudden ascent from subtropical shoreline to misty peaks makes for all manner of microclimates.

In the markets, chestnuts and peaches are piled alongside avocados, papayas and bananas. And, of course, grapes – those that haven't ended up as Madeira wine.

The island's beauty and mild climate have long attracted refugees from fierce northern weather. During the 19th and 20th centuries, Madeira was the wintering spot for the wealth and royalty of Europe. More recently, visitors have discovered the delights of deep-sea fishing (just a few metres off the coast) and the drama of walks in the interior. So today, the genteel folk who take afternoon tea at Reid's Hotel have been joined by a younger set who stride off into the mountains. But because rocky Madeira has no real beaches to boast of, it has been spared the onslaught of holiday-makers who simply want to lie in the sun, no matter where that sun might be shining.

Some 700km (438 miles) due west of the African coastline, Madeira has a surface area of 741km^2 (459sq.miles), and rises at its highest point to over 1860m (6102ft). In places it plunges sharply to the sea – Cabo Girão, to the west of the capital Funchal, is the second highest sea cliff in the world, with a drop of 589m (1932ft) to the breakers. A spine of mountains runs the length of the island and, as bad weather here comes from the north, the northern side of this jagged dragon's back is considerably wetter than the south. But centuries ago, intrepid labourers began to build levadas – water channels that cut through the mountains to irrigate the drier south side of the island. A walk along a levada wall takes you with relative ease into a mountain landscape that would otherwise require crampons and serious climbing skills; or through steep farmland that comprises stacks of tiny terraces, where the only feasible farm implements are hand-tools and a basket strapped to your back. Along the way, you might walk past banana trees, then up through mist and conifers to emerge on a rocky mountaintop, looking down on puffy cumulus clouds as if from an aeroplane. On a clear day, from Pico Ruivo – the highest point on the island – the sea is visible all around, and appears to slope downwards to the horizon – here the lone walker feels, quite literally, on top of the world.

Of the other islands in the Madeiran archipelago, only Porto Santo, 40km (25 miles) to the north is inhabited, yet it couldn't be more different from its larger sister. A dusty, tawny, low-slung island with scant vegetation, it has the one thing Madeira lacks – 8km (5 miles) of soft, sandy beach. Yet only a handful of hotels are scattered along this stretching seafront, and the island rests in detached, gentle torpor. Porto Santo's single claim to fame is that it was supposedly once home to explorer Christopher Columbus. Conflicting facts and the embellishments of legend entwine hopelessly, but it does seem that the great explorer was married to Filipa Moniz, daughter of the Captain of Porto Santo, and many believe he spent time on the island before heading to the Americas. The island's sole tourist attraction is the house that Columbus reputedly occupied.

The Desertas – three islands some 30km (19 miles) southeast of Madeira -- are, geologically speaking, just an extension of the main island and are, as their name implies, devoid of human life – only seals, seabirds and a particularly nasty variety of tarantula inhabitant these islands.

Over 250km (156 miles) to the south, closer to the Canary Islands than to Madeira itself, the rocky islets of The Selvagens (Savage Isles) are supposedly where the Scottish pirate Captain Kidd stashed his life's booty.

The Madeiran archipelago belongs to Portugal, but has special status as an Autonomous Political Region, with its own parliament and president. The first Portuguese settlers arrived on Madeira in the early 15th century. Some of the houses

Right *The steep streets of São Vicente sometimes give up the battle and turn into stairways, with hundreds of steps.*

Opposite *Funchal stretches down the slopes to the sea – a fine first view for anyone arriving on the island.*

in Funchal's Old Town – the small, single-storey ones with natural red (rather than grey) stone surrounds to the windows – very probably date back as long ago as this. The settlers found a verdant but deserted isle. 'One of the beauties of Madeira,' commented the English man of letters Sacheverell Sitwell dryly, 'is that, comparatively, it has no past... It was a virgin island. There were no aboriginal inhabitants to exterminate.' Perhaps this gentle beginning is a reason for the calm that seems to infuse the island and its people. Not that Madeira's history is entirely placid. Sugar, and later Madeira wine, made Madeirans rich, and as a result, the island was ravaged by pirates. It was also used as a strategic refuelling spot for sea journeys to the Americas by both the British and the Spanish – the large fort that overlooks Funchal, as well as Fortaleza de São Tiago in the Old Town, were both built during the Spanish occupation.

Portugal may have owned Madeira for the best part of five centuries, but the British have been residents for three and have been such a weighty presence that, at times, Westminster viewed Madeira more as a colony than as foreign territory. British families were behind the boom in the Madeiran wine trade, which had reached its peak in the 18th and 19th centuries. A fortified wine that packs more punch than sherry yet is not as sticky as port, Madeira was once one of the most popular wines in the world. A glass of Madeira sealed the signing of the American Declaration of Independence, it was the favourite tipple of Shakespeare's cheery drunkard Falstaff, and is still used to toast anyone offered the Freedom of the City of London. Madeira slipped out of fashion last century, but is making a gradual come-back as a new generation discovers the rich burnt-nutty flavours of the finest wines. Many of the best brands still bear the names of their original British makers, such as Blandy, Cossart and Miles, and descendants of those families are still cornerstones of island social life – change on islands happens slowly.

This cosy conservatism is perhaps most evident in Funchal, which has a safe and comfortably old-fashioned mood. Women walk alone at night, street crime is virtually nonexistent, families still socialize together – on a Saturday night at a seafront café you'll see brothers and sisters joint-dating

Above left *Patterned flowerbeds are a Madeiran specialty, such as these in the Botanical Gardens high above Funchal.*
Left *Colourful flowers, fresh fruit and vegetables – the island's speciality – fill the farmers' marketplace in Funchal all year round.*
Opposite *The road winds down to Ponta do Sol ('Sun Point'), so named as it's the islanders' favourite spot for viewing the sunset.*

their friends. Funchal is also the dining-out focal point of the island, where people cram into tiny restaurants in the Old Town to tuck into the local favourite of espada – a sleek, succulent deep-sea fish – with fried banana. The city is also the setting for Madeira's three most colourful celebrations – Carnival in February, the annual Flower Festival at the end of April, with local bands, folk-dancing and a parade of flower-laden floats; and the explosion of fireworks on Old Year's Night that attracts a flotilla of cruise ships to view the spectacle from offshore.

Most of the wicker work and 'Madeiran lace' (finely wrought embroidery, some of it of exceptional quality), still made by hand in homes around the island, make its way to outlets in the city. Funchal harbours a few cultural treasures, too – churches with centuries-old carved ceilings and priceless *azulejos* (coloured tiles); historical family houses, and a stash of 15th- and 16th-century Flemish paintings, once owned by sugar barons and seemingly unnoticed by art historians in the outside world.

Above *From Pico Arieiro to Pico Ruivo you can walk a path that's on top of the world.*
Opposite *Triangular thatched houses from Santana in the north have become a symbol of Madeira.*

Nearly half of the island's population lives in the capital. People venturing out of Funchal do so more for walks, gardens and scenery than to visit other towns, though some villages do have their allure. Jardim do Mar, the appropriately named 'Garden of the Sea' perches on rocks on the west coast amid tangles of bougainvillea, passion flowers and geraniums; at Câmara de Lobos nearby, boat builders carve out fishing craft in much the same way as they've done for generations. Porto Moniz in the north boasts a series of volcanic tidal pools, ideal for family swimming outings; while at the heart of the island, the hamlet of Curral das Freiras – surrounded by fierce cliffs, and until fairly recently accessible only on foot – still inspires sight-seers' awe, both when viewed from above and among those who have wound down through hairpin bends to recover with a glass of the local cherry-based firewater with the villagers below.

Footpaths and the network of levadas will take walkers across the island – from the empty, windy plateau of Paúl da Serra along lonely cliff tops and to the heart of jagged gorges and the primeval forest of the national park at Quiemada, thick with ironwood, laurel and Madeiran mahogany. Here ferns, flowers and creepers crowd between the trees, soft mosses and lichens fill the gaps, birdsong filters through the leaves, and with every breath you seem to catch a different fragrance. For those who prefer their nature a little more tamed, the outer reaches of Funchal abound in glorious gardens, many of them open to the public. The Botanical Gardens offer ferns, orchids and indigenous plants; at the Monte Palace Tropical Garden a little further up the hill, there are cycads and protea that grow hardly anywhere else out of their native South Africa, while the gardens at Quinta Palheiro Ferreiro – the Blandy family home – steal the show entirely with camellia trees over 10m (33ft) high, jungle-sized tree-ferns and an abundance of rare blooms.

Not only vigorous walkers get to appreciate the scenery. Considerable European Union investment in Madeira in recent years has meant that the narrow roads, at times barely a vehicle wide which once wound tortuously around the island's mountainous terrain, have in many cases been upgraded or replaced. This has been done with acute sensitivity, using tunnels rather than crashing across attractive countryside. So, although the adventurous can use the old routes, the less brave of heart can take the low road, emerging on the other side of the island within minutes. And the roads reach almost everywhere – this must be one of the few places where you can take a taxi from the city centre to a mountain-top above the clouds.

'Madeira,' noted one 19th-century traveller admiringly, 'ensures almost every European comfort with every tropical luxury'. Today's visitors would be inclined to agree. A landscape that is pretty much unassailable, and a populace that seems inherently careful and conservative have, despite the odd patch of ugly new building, preserved the essence of Madeira. Tropical

fruit and exotic flora come in a distinctly Old World setting. For years Madeira has had a slightly fuddy-duddy image. Like its wines, the island has slipped from fashion. In both instances the wind is beginning to change. While the mild climate and gentle pace of life may lull visitors into indolence, and still attract the more elderly traveller, the network of levadas lure the energetic out of the towns to be rewarded by quite another aspect of the island. The grandees who made Madeira a fashionable resort for over two centuries are a dying breed, and the absence of good beaches has saved the island from the worst excesses of package-holiday tourism. Today Madeira rests somewhere between the two worlds. It remains a haven for well-off retired folk who require life to be calm and unchallenging, yet is fast becoming one of Europe's prime destinations for walkers.

Belle-Île

ROGER ST PIERRE

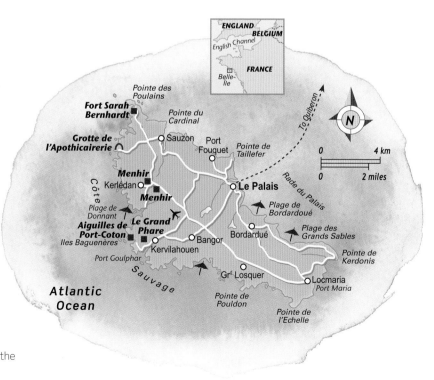

The very name augurs well: Belle-Île (Beautiful Island). That might seem a terrible misnomer as the ferryboat pitches and tosses over white-capped waves, and all that can be seen from the sky through the drizzle is a far-off hulking, flat-topped grey landmass. But the weather in these parts is nothing if not capricious, and within seconds of landing on the island the rain stops, the broodingly dark clouds are swept from the sky and the gaily painted houses of Le Palais bask under bright and welcoming sunlight.

Belle-Île en Mer, to give this diminutive French Atlantic coast island its correct title, is set 13km (8 miles) off Brittany's Quiberon Peninsula. Covering 53km² (33sq.miles), it's essentially a flat plateau, covered with heather and dotted with picturesque whitewashed cottages, with their hallmark blue-painted doors and shutters. What gives the island its hypnotic appeal is the rugged granite coastline and the succession of sheltered little valleys winding inland from secluded coves, beaches, sand dunes and dizzying cliffs. Here grow wild figs and myrtle, hydrangeas and hortensias, masses of wildflowers and sprawling blackberry bushes. While the wind can be fearsome, often reaching 160km per hour even in high summer, the climate is mild year round, and sheltered spots are lush and bounteous.

Centuries ago, the island's Roman name was Vindilis, but it was corrupted to Guedel in the Middle Ages. The monks of Quimperle's Abbey of Ste Croix passed the island to the Retz family in 1572. By 1718, this strategically placed spot was in the hands of King Louis XV. It is often said of the French king's great military architect Sébastien le Pretre de Vauban, that no fortress he built was ever conquered while none he besieged withstood the onslaught. That's not quite true: in 1761 red-coated British marines stormed and seized the capital Le Palais's mighty star-shaped citadel. In all fairness, Vauban had warned his royal master that the defences would be inadequate unless he was given sufficient budget to fortify both sides of this great natural harbour. Later French governments saw sense and did precisely that.

After two years in British hands, the island was exchanged for Nova Scotia at the end of the wars that saw the French abandon their Canadian colonies.

Those French Canadians who refused to swear allegiance to the British crown were asked to leave, in none too polite terms. In the resultant diaspora, most of these Acadians headed south, establishing Louisiana's distinctive Cajun culture. But numerous families chose instead to be repatriated to France and in 1765, some 363 souls wound up on Belle-Île. They proved highly industrious, establishing smallholdings and fishing the rough Atlantic waters.

Belle-Île is a place of four distinct seasons, and it can be said that they are all experienced in one day — and twice! Only during the August school holidays does the population soar from 4800 to 35,000, but for romantics the best times to visit are spring, with its carpets of wildflowers, and autumn, when heather turns from purple to brown.

This is where President Mitterand escaped the political milieu of bustling Paris. The actress Sarah Bernhardt, the writer Marcel Proust and the painter Claude Monet were drawn here too. Bernhardt wafted in every summer for 30 years, while Monet arrived here in 1886, produced 10 paintings of the little fishing village of Kervilahouen, then went on to paint 39 impressions of the island's rugged coast-

line. This is truly a magnet for artists, dreamers and romantics; an island for families too — and many have holiday homes here. Yachtsmen love it, though the currents can be fearsome and jagged rocks await the reckless.

Many choose to ramble the 90km (56 miles) of unspoiled coastline — Belle-Île measures 20km (12.4 miles) by 9km (5.6 miles) — while the humble bicycle is a great way to get around, though the oft-times near gale-force winds can demand bottom gear even on the flattest of roads.

Beachcombing quickly becomes a passion; mussels, whelks, periwinkles and clams are there for the plucking in myriad rock pools A bounteous *plateau des fruits de mer* will set them on a bed of seaweed and ice, accompanied by garlicky mayonnaise and locally fished lobster, crab, langoustine, oysters and those odd little crustaceans known as pousse pieds, which look like tiny elephant feet.

Right *Lighthouses abound, adding charm but serving a practical purpose in dangerously rocky waters that are often lashed by Atlantic storms. This pair guards the entrance to the harbour at Le Palais.*

Opposite *Still an active commercial fishing base, the sheltered haven of Sauzon is filled with leisure craft. Lobster and oysters are almost always on the menu in bistros.*

Your wallet needs to be rather thicker than on the mainland, for most things have to be brought across aboard the clanking ferryboat, which several times a day plies the often rough channel from Quiberon.

Sadly, on this far-flung outpost of Europe's mystical Celtic fringe, the Breton language is near dead, but culture and traditions survive. On special occasions you might even see an older lady in national costume, trimmed with ornate lacework.

The cuisine has a strong local flavour too: savoury and sweet crêpes and strong Breton cider, plus butter churned from the milk of plump island cows fed on lush grass from the sheltered valleys – or Rias as the locals call them.

If pedalling or hiking smacks too much of effort, hire a beach buggy – beware, there's no protection when it rains – or a more practical small saloon. There's not even much need for a map: while there's a web of peaceful lanes to explore, the views are usually wide open and you will never be far from a glimpse of the sea which will enable you to re-calibrate your bearings.

Driving puts you anywhere on the island within 20 minutes, though an extra half-hour will probably be needed for the walk down the winding cliffpath to that chosen dream beach.

The choice might well be Sauzon, set on its protective fjord-like inlet. The selection of eateries in this tiny port is of plenty proportions, or you might prefer to buy fresh fish from the fishermen and take it home for supper. Should you be renting one of the many holiday homes here, perhaps you'll find a traditional open stove on

Above left *Sand dunes and gorse-studded heathlands back the sweeping sandy beach at Plage de Donnat where surfers enjoy the Atlantic swell.*

Above right *Where the surging waves of the Atlantic meet the rock of Belle-Île en Mer, the latter has had to surrender to the sea. Over millions of years the rock has been sculpted and shaped, creating a shoreline of pinnacles and cliffs, spray and foam, and havens for sea birds that can nest safely, high above the pounding waves.*

which you can cook before retiring to a languorous sleep in a wooden box bed, which snuggles around you like a cocoon while you listen to the moan of the wind and the far-off crashing of waves.

Mornings almost always seem bright on Belle-Île, as if the world and its weather are turning over a new leaf. It's the time for strong, fresh brewed coffee and a walk along the beach, maybe on the broad, sweeping strand of Plage des Grands Sables or on the other, more rugged side of the island at Plage de Donnant, backed by its sand dunes and sandwiched between jagged offshore pinnacles of rock.

No wonder that in 1836 they built the towering 52m (171ft) Grand Phare lighthouse here. Its 213 granite steps, topped by a stretch of wrought-iron staircase, will open lungs and set pulses racing, but the stunning views make the effort worthwhile.

Île de Groix lies to the northwest. To the east can be spotted the smaller sister islands of Île de Houat and Île de Hoëc and the long, extending finger of the Quiberon Peninsula beckons from the mainland.

Tarry awhile, though. Race round for a day and you might think you've seen it all, but those who return year after year know this is an island of hidden secrets and constant surprises.

Inland Bangor is a quiet little agricultural village, while a giddyingly steep lane down from tiny Locmaria arrives at the secret cove of Port Maria, a smuggler's dream where bushes and ferns reach right down to the waterside. Stumble across a gaunt concrete remnant of Hitler's vaunted Atlantic Wall defence; happen by chance on a 'Pardon' religious parade; search for starfish and anemones in the rock pools, or stand and watch the colour and whirring wheels of the annual round-the-island bicycle race – just one of a season-long programme of festivals and events.

There's a welcome lack of blatant commercialism, fast-foods and neon. The locals are more than happy to share their island, and tourism is vital for economic survival but this is a living, working community with an inner desire to follow its own fortune. Treat her kindly and Belle-Île en Mer will repay many times over. Walk the paths past lonely stands of pine, swim in surprisingly clear waters, marvel at the wildflowers and abundance of bird life and be thankful for the interplay of man and nature. But never forget that this is a fragile landscape that deserves your respect.

Left *Set on a steep-sided inlet on the island's landward side, Le Palais might be a small village, but it definitely displays the elegance and style of a vibrant provincial capital.*

Jersey

ROWLAND MEAD

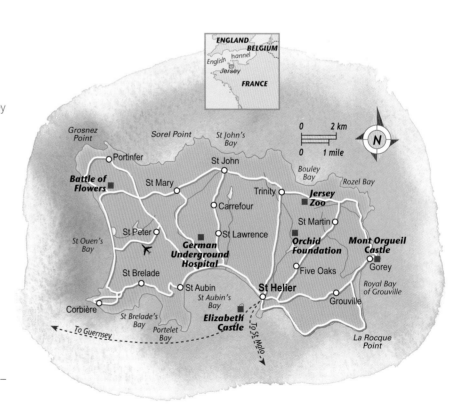

Seen from the air, the almost rectangular island of Jersey appears to have a scalloped outline, caused by the juxtaposition of bays and headlands, giving the promise of spectacular scenery. Down at ground level, the visitor is not disappointed. Beetling granite cliffs, particularly in the north of the island, are interspersed with small coves and bays, lined with crescents of yellow sand crying out for exploration and relaxation. In contrast, the extreme west of the island is lined with sand dunes backed with marshes and nature reserves. The seas are subject to the biggest tidal ranges in the world, with waves rising as high as 12m (39ft) during Spring tides. Inland, quiet country lanes lined with stone walls meander between fields containing local specialties, such as the Jersey Royal potatoes and the deer-like Jersey cattle. Jersey is the largest of the Channel Islands – the others are Guernsey, Alderney, Sark and Herm –

belonging to the United Kingdom but close to the French coast, which is a mere 19km (12 miles) away. It covers 116km² (45sq.miles), sloping gently from north to south. Jersey has a population of around 85,000, roughly half of which live in the capital St Helier. Once linked physically to France, the Channel Islands became detached from the mainland after the Ice Age, when melting ice caused the sea levels to rise. Jersey was the last of the islands to be separated, and this may be the reason why Jersey has a wider range of animals and reptiles, such as moles and toads, than the other islands. (The inhabitants of Jersey are known irreverently as 'toads' by the other Channel islanders.)

The history of Jersey is long and fascinating. There is evidence that many centuries ago the island was once inhabited by Gauls, and later, around AD56, the Romans occupied the island. Most of the parishes, such as St Helier and St Martin, were named after Celtic saints during this period.

A landmark date in the history of the Channel Islands is 933, when the islands were taken over by the Normans. As William, King of Normandy, was later to become King of England, there began a link to the English throne that has endured until today. There were, however, many hiccups along the way, as the French made repeated attempts to regain the islands. The most serious threat came in 1781, when Baron de Rullecourt invaded Jersey. The Governor surrendered the island, but the Jersey militia were having none of this and took on the invaders in Royal Square in St Helier. It is claimed that the battle lasted barely 10 minutes before the French were sent packing. A century later, Napoleon posed an even bigger threat, but a series of defensive towers built around the island proved a sufficient deterrent to the Frenchman.

A foreign power eventually succeeded in occupying the islands, when in 1940 during World War II, the Germans arrived. This was the only British territory to fall to the enemy. The five years of occupation were a traumatic time for the islanders; many were subjected to slavery, deportation and, towards the end of the

war, starvation. Collaborators with the enemy were ostracized and young women who fraternized with German soldiers had their heads shaved. Ironically, many of the fortifications built by the Germans are tourist attractions today.

The Channel Islands are divided into two bailiwicks: one of which is Jersey, with its own parliament known as a States Assembly. This is made up of a number of elected senators and deputies who reach decisions simply by consensus. It is an extraordinary fact that the Jersey parliament has no political parties, cabinet or prime minister – surely the only country in the world where such a system of government prevails. The official language of Jersey is English, but 'Frenchness' pervades the island. Many of the old established families have French names. Physical features such as hills, headlands and rivers are named in French, while the vernacular architecture of the island has strong echoes of Normandy. Street names are often seen in both languages, with the French version frequently the more interesting. The people of Jersey, however, remain fiercely British in their outlook.

International finance has become Jersey's biggest industry in recent years, and its low rate of personal and corporate taxation has made the island a popular offshore tax haven. A more traditional industry is agriculture, which has supported the Jersey economy for centuries. The mild climate has encouraged the production of

Right *Enjoy a cocktail and socialize at one of the colourful open-air cafés on the promenade along the shore of the St Brelade coast.*

Opposite *Floodlit at night, the .formidable Mt Orgueil Castle dominates the charming fishing port of Gorey – parts of the castle date back to the 13th century.*

early flowers and vegetables for export, as they can be harvested well in advance of similar crops on the British mainland. Jersey Royal potatoes are particularly popular, while broccoli and tomatoes have become big earners in recent years. Some crops are grown in the small open fields, while others are grown under glass. Sheep provide the wool for the famous Jersey sweaters. Much of Jersey's farmland has remained unspoiled and unchanged, due largely to the island's strict planning laws. Green Zones and Sensitive Landscape Areas prohibit development, while in Agricultural Priority Zones, only farming is allowed. Crisscrossing the farmland is a network of 40 miles of 'Green Lanes', which give priority to farm vehicles, walkers, cyclists and horse riders. The fishing industry, in contrast, is in decline, due to decreasing fish stocks and subsequent European Union Conservation regulations.

The tourist industry offers the best hope for the future. Jersey is blessed with warm summers and winters that are milder than both the English and French mainlands, prolonging the tourist season. There is a wide selection of accommodation available, ranging from five-star hotels to intimate bed-and-breakfast establishments. Apart from the gentle scenery and clean sandy beaches, there are numerous attractions to tempt the visitor. Many have connections with Jersey's historic past, such as the magnificently sited Mont Orgueil Castle at Gorey, dating back to the 13th century. Once a prison, it has for many centuries been the residence of the governors of the island, one of whom was Sir Walter Raleigh (1600–03). The English monarch

Charles II spent part of his exile at Mont Orgueil as a guest of the Governor George de Carteret, who as a reward received land in America that became New Jersey.

The German Occupation of Jersey from 1940 until 1945 is remembered in a number of sites. The German Occupation Tapestry is located in St Helier in an old warehouse next to the harbourside Maritime Museum. It consists of a series of panels, each embroidered by a different parish, illustrating the story of the Occupation, from the invasion to the liberation. Nearby is the Island Fortress Occupation Museum. Here there is a display of military memorabilia and a video gives a graphic description of island life during the Occupation. There are also Occupation connections displayed at St Helier's Military Museum and at Elizabeth Castle, which the Germans reinforced as part of their 'Atlantic Wall'. By far the most atmospheric and poignant, however, is the German War Tunnels and Underground Hospital at St Lawrence, just to the northwest of St Helier. The complex of tunnels was originally built by the forced labour of assorted Jews, Poles and Russian prisoners-of-war, who were reportedly treated little better than animals. It was originally built to be bomb-proof barracks and an ammunition store. When it was clear that the war was being lost, the Germans converted the tunnels into an underground hospital, equipping it with an operating theatre, mortuary, X-ray room and nursing quarters. On display are films, photographs, newspaper cuttings and personal memorabilia giving a chilling indication of the suffering and trauma experienced during this period of Jersey's history,

when the enemy was literally living at the door. Visitors, on entering the complex, are given an identity card – a facsimile of a real card used by islanders during the Occupation. At the end of the tour, you can identify your card owner by photographs and details on a wall display. It is quite a shock to find, say, that your card owner, a dark-haired young girl of around 24, is identified as a shaven-headed collaborator. It is no surprise to learn that the German Underground Hospital was voted one of the best new tourist attractions in Britain in 2001.

There are scores of other attractions on Jersey, and all are accessible, as it is easy to drive around the whole bailliwick in a day. The capital, St Helier, is a vibrant town and well worth a visit. It had its main growth in the 19th century, but recent years have seen a re-development of the waterfront, the pedestrianization of the shopping centre and a construction of a bypass that has relieved congestion in the central area.

Undoubtedly the most famous attraction on the island is Jersey Zoo. Located in the parish of Trinity in the north of the island, the zoo was set up in 1963 by the naturalist and writer Gerald Durrell. The aim of the zoo is to research and breed rare and endangered species. In this it has achieved considerable

Above left *The annual flower show and its procession of flower-festooned floats is a highlight of the year.*

Above right *Jersey has a network of walking routes as shown in this view of the coastal footpath near breathtaking Portelet and the Ille de Guerdain.*

Opposite *The German Underground Hospital, which was built during WWII, is now a well-known museum and Jersey's most vivid reminder of the wartime occupation. The hospital's original German name was Hohlgangsanlage 8.*

success, providing animals for other zoos and returning numerous threatened animals to the wild. Many of the animals roam freely through the 4ha (10 acres) of woodland, gardens and landscaped enclosures. The congenial atmosphere certainly aids the breeding successes that the zoo has achieved. All the family, particularly children, will enjoy this visit. Also in Trinity parish is the Orchid foundation, which was set up in 1958 by the horticulturist Eric Young. Unlike the zoo, its understated approach is not designed to attract the family, but is unashamedly meant to appeal to orchid enthusiasts and plant-lovers in general. Over 20,000 orchids are displayed in a purpose built exhibition complex, making it probably the finest private collection in the world. Many visitors return to Jersey year after year, timing their visit to coincide with one of the island's feast of festivals. The most impressive festival is the Battle of Flowers, which takes place on the second Thursday in August. It was started in 1902 to celebrate the coronation of Edward VII. Up to 30 florally bedecked floats parade along Victoria Avenue before being broken up by the onlookers who pelt each other with the flowers to the accompaniment of fireworks – a crazy end to one of the top 10 floral parades in the world!

So how will the island of Jersey shape out in the future? Will its financial industry's status as a tax haven survive? How will the farming industry cope with competition from fruit and vegetables produced more cheaply abroad? Will the tourist industry survive as cheap travel makes more exotic destinations within reach of the ordinary person?

One thing is certain, an island that came through five years of enemy occupation, with its deprivation, humiliations and near starvation, has a good chance of dealing with anything that the future can throw up.

Isle of Skye

GRAHAM SIMMONS

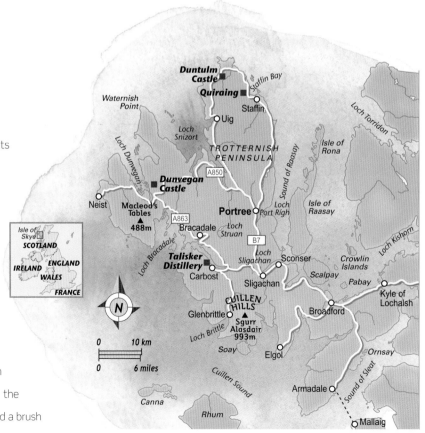

ew places on earth awaken such lyrical longing as the Isle of Skye. Its colours dazzle the eye – lime-green moss contrasts starkly against weathered black rock, yellow dock spikes and bright red hawthorn berries seem to glow, and the emerald shades of fir and pine trees and grassy meadows offer vistas of verdant green. When a seabird alights on a cliff, its plumage shimmers in a dazzling iridescent kaleidoscope of colour.

In the village square of Portree, unofficial capital of the island, a lone piper entertains passers-by with his repertoire; the band accompanying him follows with another tune. The stirring music of the Scottish Highlands is haunting, and it is still possible to feel it evoking the soft patter of rain on heather, and multicoloured clouds soaring over craggy peaks. On Skye, even the skies take on a mystical quality, as though a celestial landscape artist has dipped a brush in the heather and used it to paint the clouds. It offers an ever-changing spectacle of vivid shades, from pink to mauve to kirk-purple, that tint the shadows reflected on the ground.

An upbeat air of newfound cultural pride is evident all over the Isle of Skye, with close to half the population now speaking Gaelic. The Aros Centre, just out of Portree on a scenic arm of Loch Port Rígh, is dedicated to this full-scale Gaelic revival. The first attraction encountered by the visitor is the 'Gaelic Alphabet Trail', a re-creation of the days when different trees were used to teach the Gaelic alphabet to children (for example, 'A' stands for Ailm (Elm), 'B' for Beith (Birch), and so on).

Indoors, *The Aros Experience* is a stirring multimedia presentation of the history of Skye, including the times of the infamous 'Clearances'. Prince Charles Edward Stuart – better known as 'Bonnie Prince Charlie' or the Young Pretender – escaped to Skye in 1745 after the Battle of Culloden, when the Highland army was defeated by English forces commanded by the Duke of Cumberland.

The collapse of the Highland uprising set in train an orgy of revenge by the English, who set out to punish the islanders for their support of the uprising. Subsequently, during the 'Clearances' of the 1800s, thousands of 'Skyelanders' were forcibly removed from their crofts, often with the connivance of the Highland chiefs, and some were sent to work as slaves on the plantations of North Carolina.

Many others emigrated to Canada, or to Australia, principally to the Western District of Victoria. With the assistance of the Highland and Island Emigration Society, the barque *Georgiana* arrived in the southern Australian city of Geelong in 1852, with a load of 357 people from the Isle of Skye. Another ship, the *SS Arabian*, carrying a load of Skyelanders, arrived in nearby Portland in 1854. Most of the migrants spoke only Scots Gaelic and, even today, the Comun na Feine pub in Geelong is home to the descendants of Gaelic-speakers from the Isle of Skye.

Right *The impressive Skye bridge connects the Isle of Skye with the mainland, so you can just hop into your car and be on the island in no time.*
Opposite *Looking out from the Cuillins across Loch Scavaig, a coastal path snakes its way from Elgol to Loch Coruisk in the heart of the Cuillin Hills.*

After the 1745 rising, the clan chieftains of the Highlands and Islands were stripped of their hereditary powers. Traditional Highland dress was banned, as was the speaking of Scots Gaelic, which had been the language of the islanders for over 1600 years. When Samuel Johnson and James Boswell visited Skye in 1773 they spoke of a population downtrodden and demoralized. Only at the Napier Commission of 1893 were the crofters' grievances heard for the first time.

Following a prolonged decline, the population of Skye is now rising rapidly for the first time in 150 years, and many island children are being taught in Gaelic as a first language. Throughout the Isle of Skye, a huge resurgence of interest in Gaelic music has also taken place, with the Highland Festival, or *Feis an Eilein* – held from the last week in May to the second week of June – attracting visitors from around the world. Near Armadale, in the south of the Island, a Gaelic language college, Sabhal Mor Ostaig, has performed wonders in reviving Scots Gaelic.

Getting to the Isle of Skye is not difficult. From Aberdeen, regular rail services run to Kyle of Lochalsh, from where there are regular bus connections, across the impressive Skye Road bridge, to Portree.

A very pleasant route back to the Scottish mainland is by ferry from the southern Skye town of Armadale to Mallaig, where you connect with the scenic

train service – a steam train runs on Sunday afternoons in summer – to Fort William and then on to Glasgow.

From the Lochalsh road bridge landing on Skye, the road hugs the coast and then traverses the picturesque Loch Sligachan, before veering inland, with spectacular views from the village of Sconser towards the Isle of Raasay. The island is now a nature conservation zone, with the Raasay Outdoor Centre offering lessons in rock climbing, sailing, kayaking and a host of other activities.

But Raasay was not always so tranquil. After the island sent a contingent of pipers and troops to fight on the losing side at the Battle of Culloden in 1745, avenging English forces responded by ransacking Raasay, destroying most of its buildings and razing crops. Bonnie Prince Charlie spent a 'miserable' night here during his flight to France after the battle. During the mid-1800s, the Clearances were particularly strongly enforced on the island.

The best way to explore this strangely shaped island, with its many isolated peninsulas, is undoubtedly by rental car. Car hire is fairly inexpensive, especially if the cost is divided among a group of people. In fact, having your own car is virtually *de rigueur* in these parts as the bus service can be a trifle erratic. Hiring your own vehicle enables you to explore at will.

If you wish to begin your exploration with a spectacular destination, head for the Cuillin Hills; it has the best hiking in the whole of Scotland. The road from Portree to the Cuillins becomes steeper at Sligèachan (Sligachan) and visitors will notice that all the road signs are in Gaelic first, English second. You can park your a car at

Glenbrittle, at the dead-end of the Cuillen road, and then set off on one of several walking trails that lead up the ridge. Following the trail that takes you up to the brooding Loch an Fhir Bhallaich, leaves behind truly spectacular views over the Loch Brittle inlet.

The Cuillin Hills make for sensational walking. The lochs and corries (hollows that once saw the birth of glaciers) that dot the 13km (8-mile) range ensure that every step brings something new to savour and enjoy. Along the hiking paths, heather and sedges compete for space, while the tallest peak, Sgurr Alasdair, is just less than 1000m (3281ft) high; the air nevertheless feels cool and bracing.

It's difficult to leave the Cuillins, but the rest of Skye still beckons. Naturally, it's hard to resist an invitation to visit the Talisker single-malt distillery, at the very west

Above Dunvegan Castle is still in good repair and has been the home of the MacLeod family for 800 years.

Above left While the Cuillin Hills offer possibly the best hiking in the whole of Scotland, a walk along Loch Sligachan is also as rewarding.

of the island near the village of Carbost. The distillery, built in 1830 despite the fiery protestations of the then parish minister Rev Robert MacLeod, is described by its parent company as one of just six producers of 'classic malts'. Talisker is a superb brew, at once both peaty and smoky, as though the essence of the soil has seeped up through the soles of the taster's boots as far as the tastebuds – or beyond.

The road northwest of Talisker (the A863) hugs the coast and offers spectacular views of sea and rugged coastline. In the quaint little village of Bracadale, overlooking the beautiful Loch Struan, you can refresh yourself, enjoy the view, and continue your journey around this lovely island.

At Dunvegan Castle, the gatekeeper will demand an entry fee, but it's well worth it. The interior of the castle might not seem to be anything special, but the grounds are superb, and the view of the ocean from the castle forecourt is riveting.

Crossing a saddle to the dramatic Loch Snizort via the A850, the road heads

north along the coast of the Trotternish Peninsula. The entrance to the fishing town of Uig is marked by a striking broch, a prehistoric stone tower. At these latitudes, the Old Norse place names recall the Viking invaders who marauded these shores a millennium ago.

In the 13th century, the Norse became settlers rather than raiders, at places still bearing names like Fiskavaig, Herebost, Hunglader and Monkstadt.

Twisting and turning upon itself, the road north of Uig traverses some of Skye's most spectacular scenery. Near the ruins of Duntulm Castle, where Viking long-

Above *Cheviot sheep grazing on grassland along Duntulm Bay. Their wool is the most important 'ingredient' in Harris Tweed.*
Opposite *Buildings overlooking the harbour in Portree display the solid architectural style typical of the west of Scotland.*
Opposite left *The steep, slippery slopes of Kilt Rock on the Trottenish Peninsula are dramatic and dizzying, and a perfect location for sighting the rare Sea Eagle.*

ships once rode at anchor, the Conor family now raises Cheviot sheep. The wool is a key ingredient in the much-prized Harris Tweed.

The Isle of Skye is certainly scenic, but it is a scenery that has been created over millions of years. The harsh winter weather and its attendant ice and snow has shaped, cracked and cut the landscape and the island itself, creating the gem that is the Isle of Skye of today. North of Duntulm, as you round the northern tip of the Trottenish peninsula, even the 'by then mild' breeze abates. In the lee of Mt Quiraing,

fishing boats bob nonchalantly in Staffin Bay. Staffin is Skye's second largest settlement, boasting a 'Vegetarian Internet' bed-and-breakfast establishment, almost as though the two somehow go hand-in-hand.

Back in Portree, as the sun sets over the harbour, the picture-postcard shops and houses that line the waterfront glow with a golden radiance. And at night, Portree comes to life: the Island Inn has great live music, while the Isles Inn and the Bosville Hotel also attract crowds of revellers.

Early in the morning, a red tinge warms the chimney tops along the quay of Portree Harbour. When it's time to leave the Isle of Skye — not as Bonnie Prince Charlie did, in a hasty retreat — but with a the sadness of bidding farewell to a new-found friend — the visitor experiences a real feeling of nostalgia. But it's tinged with a warm glow of certainty...

There will be another time, and the Skye Boat Song will never sound so heart-rending as when you are in that frame of mind!

Rügen

ANTHONY LAMBERT

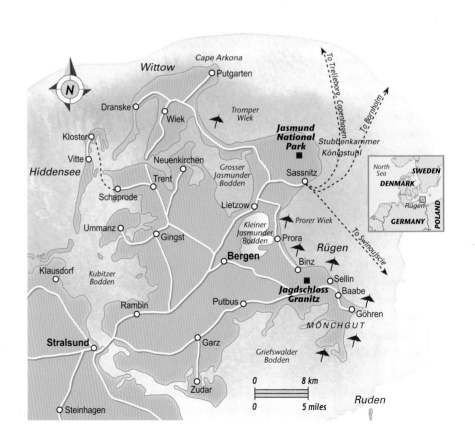

Standing on the end of the pier at Binz, listening to the gentle lap of water and gazing eastwards towards the tree-crowned headland, dark against the Prussian blue moonlit sky, it's easy to see why the German romantic painter Caspar David Friedrich was drawn to this island, along with numerous other painters and writers. Thomas Mann came here to relax, and Elizabeth von Arnim became so enthralled with the place that one of her series of 'Elizabeth' novels incorporates her travels around the island. Brahms, Einstein, Bismarck and East Germany's last leader Erich Honecker also came here for a holiday.

Yet Germany's largest island seems to be a secret the Germans want to keep. Few outside the Baltic countries have heard of Rügen, never mind visited the island that has delighted generations of Germans since 1815, when 167 years of Swedish rule came to an end and the island became part of Prussia.

Access probably has much to do with it; it takes four hours by train from Hamburg to reach the Rügendamm, the causeway that links the Hanseatic mainland port of Stralsund with the island. Since Rügen remains so popular with Germans – it is unwise to leave accommodation to chance in July and August – there is little incentive to promote its pleasures to foreigners.

Nor would the train journey bisecting the island to the principal port of Sassnitz be enough to explain the island's appeal, though historians will appreciate that Lenin came this way in 1917 on his way from Switzerland through Germany to Russia; the coach that carried him can be seen at Sassnitz station. The scenery is pleasant enough, and the spires of Bergen, the island's capital, indicate a town worth exploring. But much of the island's attraction, in common with most islands, lies in its astonishingly varied coast. This is not so surprising when you learn that this 976km² (377sq.mile) island has a coastline of 574km (359 miles); so deeply indented are its inlets and estuaries that some form large inland lagoons like the Grosser Jasmunder Bodden.

But to discover the less well-known aspects of the island, you need to copy Elizabeth von Arnim and take to its byways. She acquired large-scale maps and set about exploring Rügen's backroads with military thoroughness. Today she would probably choose the network of dedicated bicycle routes that makes it a pleasure to use this ideal mode of transport for leisurely bumbling around, especially on Rügen where hills are seldom either long or steep. Gliding through the island's glorious beech woods, between avenues of lime trees or among yellow fields of rape, you can enjoy the sounds and scents of nature, something motorists deny themselves.

The most popular resorts are on the east coast at Binz, Sellin and Göhren. Besides sandy beaches, all three resorts have piers offering boat excursions to attractions along the coast, such as the neighbouring islands of Usedom and Oie, passing chalk cliffs of such splendour that they are known as the Chalk Coast. Göhren has four museums, including an old coastal freighter drawn up on the south beach that tells the story of its trade around Rügen. It is also one end of a narrow gauge railway that performs an important public transport role, linking a series of tourist attractions, as well as delighting young and old with its characterful steam locomotives. Pausing to collect passengers at the large resort of Baabe, the Rasender Roland (Racing Roland) climbs

Right The station at Binz has been restored to its former glory and is an example of the Bäderarchitektur style of architecture.
Opposite The square in the centre of Putbus, with the war memorial, principally to the fallen of the Franco-Prussian War of 1870–1.

into the beech woods surrounding the 107m-high (351ft) Tempelberg, surmounted by a monumental hunting 'lodge'. The Jagdschloss Granitz was the fantastic creation of Prince Wilhelm Malte of Putbus (1783–1854), who left a remarkable architectural legacy in eastern Rügen.

The square Gothic Revival building, with four cylindrical corner towers, was begun in 1837 to the design of the prolific Berlin architect Karl Friedrich Schinkel and finished nine years later. It is dominated by a central round tower with a belvedere, reached by a vertigo-inducing wrought-iron staircase of 154 steps cantilevered out from the circular walls. On a clear day, visitors are rewarded with spectacular views over the eastern part of the island from the 38m-high (125ft) platform.

Continuing westwards, the railway reaches Binz, which has been transformed since the reunification of Germany in 1990. Along the waterfront, sheltered from the Baltic Sea by a belt of pines threaded by a sandy path, is a line of delightful villas built in the late 19th century in a style known as Bäderarchitektur. Its hallmark is the filigree iron- and woodwork on the ornate verandas and balconies.

The finest bequest of Prince Wilhelm Malte is the town towards the western end of the Rasender Roland, Putbus, which can also be reached by a standard gauge branch line. Resembling a small, whitewashed version of Bath in Somerset, Putbus was the last European town to be planned as a royal seat. Adjacent to the small deer park and the 70ha (173-acre) English landscape garden of Giant Sequoias over 35m (115ft) tall, is a collection of elegant neo-classical buildings set

around a market square and Circus with radiating gravel paths and avenues of carefully trained trees. Among the dazzlingly white houses and civic buildings is Rügen's only theatre, built in 1819–21 as a place of entertainment for the Prince's guests, and today it offers an admirably varied programme. Tragically, the castle was hastily demolished in 1962 by local politicians trying to impress a visiting Communist leader with their ideological commitment.

To the south of Putbus is a huge bay with the deeply etched Mönchgut (Monk's Estate) peninsula to the east, an area of gentle hills and sandy beaches and now a nature reserve. The district developed customs quite distinct from the rest of the island because the monks who owned the area from the 14th century restricted the freedom of locals to mix with their pagan Slavic neighbours. To the west of Putbus lies the oldest town on the island, Garz, which still gives a strong impression of an 18th- and 19th-century market town; its single-storey rendered houses are reminiscent of similar-sized towns in the Highlands of Scotland.

North along the coast from Binz is one of the island's few eyesores: beside 4km (2.5 miles) of beach stand rows of dreary six-storey blocks, part of a leisure centre

created by the Nazis for 20,000 visitors but now a ghost town. They defied early post-war Soviet attempts to blow them up, and they remain as a grim reminder of the austerity of totalitarian architecture. A small museum documents their history from the start of construction in 1936.

In the novel *Effi Briest*, published in 1895, Fontane's eponymous heroine is told: 'To visit Rügen means to visit Sassnitz'. The fishing and peasant village had been 'discovered' and become a fashionable resort – Brahms wrote his first symphony here in 1876. The first seaside resort on Rügen it may have been, but apart from

Opposite top *The wrought-iron stairway up the 38m (ft) tower of Jagdschloss Granitz is not for those visitors who are prone to vertigo.*

Opposite below *The view from the top of Karl Friedrich Schinkel's tower of Jagdschloss Granitz is the most panoramic on the island of Rügen.*

Below *The Racing Roland's narrow gauge line between Putbus and Göhren threads through the woods beneath the hunting lodge of Jagdschloss Granitz.*

the old town, the port lacks the appeal it once had, despite boasting the longest harbour wall in Europe, at 1444m (4737ft). From the port, boats operate to Copenhagen and the Isle of Bornholm in Denmark, Trelleborg in Sweden, and Swinoujscie (Swinemüende in Germany) in Poland. Fishing remains second to tourism as the island's main industry, and much of the fleet is based here.

To the north lies the well-wooded Jasmund National Park and one of Rügen's best-known physical features: its picturesque chalk coastline includes the jagged cliffs of the Stubbenkammer, the feature made famous by a series of paintings of this stretch of coast by Caspar David Friedrich. It and the Königstuhl (King's Chair) are excessively popular in high season; you can reach them by walking through beech woods along the coast, passing the Wissower Klinken chalk cliffs which Friedrich also painted. The King's Chair supposedly takes its name from the occasion when King Karl XIII watched a sea battle between the Swedish and Danish navies from this point. An alternative legend suggests that anyone who could climb the 117m-high (384ft) pinnacle would become king of Rügen. Inland, within the park, is the highest point on the island, the 154m (505ft) Hertaburg. The large nearby block of stone is thought to have been a Slavic sacrificial altar, like the Inca garrotting stone at Machu Picchu in Peru.

A curved finger of tidally formed land with a 10km (6.2-mile) long beach turns north along the Grosser Jasmunder Bodden to what was once the island of Wittow.

The most fertile part of Rügen, its northern extremity at Cape Arkona is endowed with two lighthouses, the older designed by Karl Friedrich Schinkel and finished in 1827. It is an extraordinary design, square in plan and built of red brick. The viewing platforms of both lighthouses offer splendid views south along the coast towards the thatched fishing village of Vitte with its whitewashed octagonal chapel, again designed by Schinkel. The plain interior is simply decorated with naïve wall paintings of fishing-village life. Near the lighthouses are the remains of the ancient fortress of Burgwall, enclosing a temple which was destroyed in 1168 by the Danish king Waldemar I, when he made himself master of the island. Rügen was then ruled by a succession of native princes, under Danish supremacy, until 1218.

Continuing around the coast to Schaprode, you can catch a ferry to Kloster, a village on the 17km (10.5-mile) long, thin island of Hiddensee, which is regarded as a part of Rügen and has been described as 'the pearl of the Baltic'. The island is traffic-free, and bicycles can be hired in Kloster. Though flat, the island and its villages have great charm. Kloster has a whitewashed church that was built in

1332 by Cistercian monks for the fishing and farming community. The naturalist playwright Gerhart Hauptmann so loved Kloster that he asked to be buried there, and the house he bought in the village with money accompanying the Nobel Prize for Literature is open to visitors. The low-ceilinged rooms are still redolent of the 1920s. It was near Kloster that a great hoard of Viking gold jewellery was discovered in the 19th century; copies are on display in a small museum of local life.

The most northerly village, Grieben, is known for its thatched houses, and Vitte is a resort as well as the administrative centre. Beyond the most southerly village of Plogshagen, the land is covered with purple heather in August. Further south still, the dunes and marshes have restricted access to allow birds to breed without human interference. Although the attractions of the coastline understandably hold many visitors for their entire stay, there are some worthwhile excursions away from the coastal belt, several of them to former country estates in varying states of restoration.

The district around Lietzow, situated on the isthmus between the Big and Little Jasmunder Boddens, has long been settled; over 20,000 stone tools and weapons have been found in the area, some dating from c3000BC. Along the shore of the larger expanse of water lies the landscape garden of Ralswick, created over a century before the château at its centre, which was built in 1894 in a largely French style, but with an occasional Dutch gable to remind you that you are not in France. The turreted and whitewashed building is now a hotel, but the grounds are open for visitors to admire the avenue of horse chestnuts, and the specimen Hungarian silver linden, pyramid oak and maple-leaf plane trees.

Ralswick Castle can be seen across the lake from another garden on the other side of Lietzow. Very different in character, Semper is a 38ha (94-acre) forest park established in the 1920s around a castle which is again now converted into a hotel. The ponds and woodland are being reclaimed after decades of neglect during which the park was a military training ground.

Close to the narrow channel between the mainland and Rügen lies an estate and landscape park that is emblematic of the transformation that has taken place on the island since reunification. Instead of blowing up country houses, the plans for the forlorn, but immensely evocative ruin of Üselitz, dating from the 16th century, envisage its restoration and adaptation into an arts centre with carefully incorporated modern architecture. The contrast with Prora could not be greater.

Left *The chalk cliffs of Jasmund, with trees growing right to their edge, are so friable that sections periodically collapse into the sea.*
Opposite *The view from the King's Seat, atop the cliffs of the Jasmund National Park, is indeed fit for a king, offering a spectacular vista of sea and sky.*

Gotland

ROGER ST. PIERRE

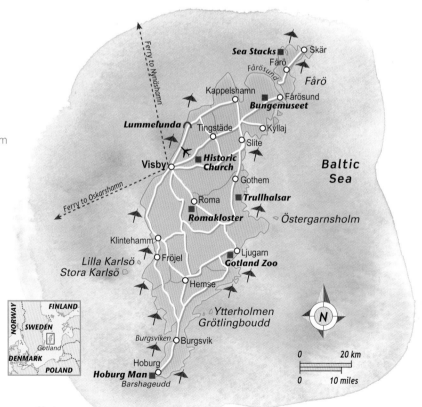

Sweden is a land of islands – some 2000 of them exist in the Stockholm archipelago alone – but for all their alluring beauty, there is one that stands out above all others, if only for its sheer size and diversity. Gotland – translate that as 'Good Land' or 'God's Land', whichever you prefer – measures 176km (109 miles) by 80km (50 miles), is home to 57,300 inhabitants, and welcomes more than 800,000 visitors each year from all over the world.

Set off Sweden's southeast coast, some 140km (87 miles) due south of Stockholm, it is one of the B7 – a multinational collection of the Baltic Sea's seven largest islands, which have come together in an effort to preserve their diverse ecology and rich culture, and have to date organized five editions of their own well-supported mini-Olympics.

This is Viking land; a place of myths and legends, a heady mix of natural beauty and intriguing history. A web of lanes and highways crisscrosses the rolling landscape, offering the dedicated explorer several thousand kilometres, and a possible lifetime, of fresh experiences, for it's an island of many secrets which are often held close to its chest.

Stone Age man first settled here 7000 years ago; yet, for all its history and tradition, this is an island with its feet firmly planted in the 21st century. Visby, the lively capital, might be a world heritage walled city, with 3.6km (2.2 miles) of medieval fortifications, but it offers all the contemporary amenities one would expect from a prosperous modern community – here fishing nets and the Internet find common cause.

Winter nights might be long and dark, but offer the amazing spectacle of the northern lights (aurora borealis) and are also compensated by healthy splodges of man-made colour on buildings that represent the gamut of fine Swedish design, ancient and modern. Red-tiled roofs are the norm, and pick up the sunshine of clear and wonderfully long summer days when it is possible to play golf long after midnight.

Beaches here range from broad and firm stretches of sand – ideal for winter walks or summer sun-worshipping – to the colourful stones of Stenkusten (The Pebble Coast). The landscape is dotted with low hills – the highest point being a mere 82m (269ft) above sea level at Lojsta Hed. And there's the occasional rauk, as Gotland's mysterious element-carved limestone standing rock formations are locally known. Major archaeological digs are unearthing a Viking harbour at Fröjel, while the cliffs and caves of offshore Lilla Karlsö – just one of Gotland's many interesting satellite islands – reveal abundant Iron Age and later historic remains.

Stora Karlsö, Gotska Sandön and, largest of them, mystical Fårö, with its famed dry stone walls and jumble of broken rocks, all beckon.

There's an enticing 800km (500 miles) of coastline in all, ranging from heathland to low cliffs. More than 10,000 guillemots and razorbills nest on the close-to-sheer headlands of Stora Karlsö, the world's second-oldest nature conservation area after Yellowstone National Park in the US. Here the sweeping beam of the 1887 lighthouse picks out fossil beaches, grassy moorlands, leafy glades and meadows full of the renowned local wild orchids, of which there are a dozen varieties.

Gotland, despite its northern latitude, is a place of flowers and shrubs and trees too, with summer window boxes adding an extra dash of colour to the abundance of wildflowers – poppies, lilies, Swedish whitebeam and a host of other species – that adorn fallow fields and line berry-filled hedgerows. Woodlands yield crops of mushrooms, including the highly prized truffle, and foster an abundance of wildlife. Nor is just there a monotony of pine – oaks, birch, elm and other hardwoods thrive here too.

Two boys stumbled on the vast Lummelunda cave system while on holiday in the summer of 1950, and still today, thousands of tourists follow their footsteps, marvelling at the dripstones – stalactites and stalagmites. They can even take their pushchairs (strollers) with them. It's an adventure for the whole family, though only the more intrepid opt for the full experience, which entails crawling through narrow tunnels and wading icy underground lakes.

Right *Level terrain and a picturesque setting make a cycling excursion with the family almost obligatory, and most enjoyable.*

Opposite *A puppy turning its head, or two teddy bears arm in arm? Visitors can read what they like into the mystical Rauker standing rocks protruding from the sea.*

At Gotland's southern extremity stands the towering limestone stack known as Hoburg Man, while the east coast, with its long beaches and juniper-clad heaths, is famed for the big skies of its sunrises.

Gotland has no sheep. Hereabouts, they are all referred to as lambs – whatever their age. Appearing on menus as glödhoppa, their succulent meat finds its way into the distinctive local cuisine, which marries the fruits of land and sea. Saffron pancakes, rich dumplings, meatballs, truffles, succulent crayfish, plump halibut, fresh Baltic herring and a no-nonsense approach to their preparation and cooking make for a healthy and flavoursome diet. The cliché 'food like mother made' takes on a new dimension.

Nearly nine per cent of all Sweden's sugar beets are grown in Gotland's rich, loamy soil. Rye and potatoes are other important crops, while pigs, poultry and both meat and dairy cattle are raised, as well as those sheep, sorry, lambs. But, as elsewhere, there's a slow drift away from agriculture, and tourism is assuming increased importance. However, this is not, thankfully, a place for holiday parks

and mass development-style sun, sea, sand and sex resorts. People go to Gotland to be close to nature, not to assail it. And many of them stay – since 1965 the island's population has increased almost every year until now 0.7 per cent of all Swedes live on what amounts to 0.8 per cent of their country's total landmass. There's little chance of the idyll being ruined though, for ecological conservation is top of the agenda for government and community alike.

It takes three hours for the high-speed ferry, skimming the waves at up to 29 knots, to cross from Nynäshamn, near Stockholm, or Oskarshamn, further south, with a total of eight crossings a day in high season.

Visby is the point of landfall. Its walls are an imposing sight. It was the trading might of the Hanseatic League which gave the city its wealth and power in the 12th and 13th centuries, and nearly 200 buildings from that golden age of the Baltics survive to this day.

Now a beautiful park, complete with duckpond, Almedalen was formerly the harbour of Visby and frames the view of the mighty walls, which stand 11m (36ft) high and have 36 surviving towers and three main gates. Through the *Kärleksporten* (The Door of Love) stands the botanical gardens, with plane trees, walnut, mulberry and fig trees, and an abundance of colourful rose bushes set beside imposing medieval ruins.

Charming little lanes radiate from the city centre, with the rose-lined *Kiskargand* (Fisherman's Lane) the most photographed. There's a grand cathedral – the imposing 12th-century Sankta Maria, which dominates the skyline – and fine churches too, including the unusual octagonal-shaped *Helgeandsruinen*.

The smell of burning plastic emanates from the shop-till-you drop attractions of craft shopping around Adelsgaten, Ostertorg and the Sankt Hans Quarter. And, when it's time to recuperate, an abundance of pavement cafés and first-rate restaurants beckon. Moreover, it's easy to avoid the tourist hordes and get lost in the maze of pretty backstreets.

The Gotland Fornsal Museum, on Strandgaten, provides an overview of 8000 years of Gotland history, while in the countryside beyond there's the Tofta Viking Village reconstruction where numerous fun events are staged. There is also the Bunge Museum, where the simple peasant existence of bygone days is brought back to life by guides wearing costumes of past centuries, walking among old thatched crofter's cottages. Pride in heritage is reflected in July's tournaments and August's Visby Medieval Week, and there's a year-round programme of arts, music, folk dance and other cultural events. A thousand-year-old cultural meeting place at the centre of the island, Roma Kungsgärd, showcases arts and crafts, from weaving to glassblowing and metalworking, as well as presenting Shakespeare in the romantic setting of a ruined monastery.

Rich in its history, content with its present and optimistic of its future, Gotland is a place where people and nature really have truly attained harmony.

Right *Visby's Medieval Week is great fun and draws thousands of visitors, as well as reminding the islanders of their rich past.*
Opposite top *Visby boasts some of the finest surviving medieval city walls in all Europe – symbols of more troubled times on this strategically sited Baltic island.*
Opposite *Before modern tourism, fishing and farming were the mainstay of Gotland's island economy – leaving behind a wealth of picturesque villages.*

Above *The lives of the islanders of Africa and the Indian Ocean have remained unchanged over the ages – unhurried and in tune with their world.*

Africa and the Indian Ocean

Maldives

WILLIAM GRAY

Forget your favourite book or desert island disc. If you could take just one possession to any of the Maldives' Crusoe-style islands make sure it's a diver's mask. To be marooned in this Indian Ocean archipelago, even on a fortnight's luxury holiday, without the means to see underwater would be pure torture.

There are 1192 islands in this, the most watery nation on earth – and each one is surrounded by a coral reef pulsing with more colour, shapes and flashing bodies than the Rio Carnival. The Maldives are hallowed water for submariners, whether you're a seasoned scuba diver or prefer your 'Cousteau moments' from the dry comfort of a glass-bottom boat.

The 26 atolls of the Maldives are strung like turquoise beads along an 850km (530 mile) necklace, some 600km (375 miles) off the southwest tip of India. Of the 115,300km² (44,500sq.miles) of official Maldivian territory, only 298km² (115sq.miles) is land. That's less than

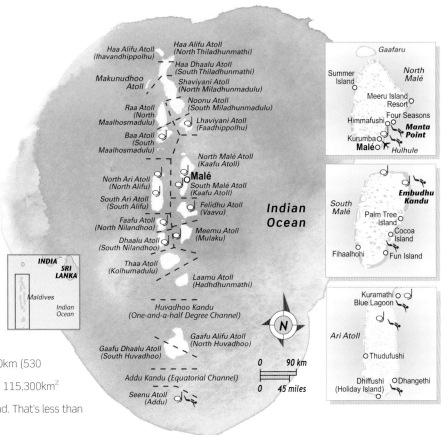

one per cent. In fact, at a scale of 1:300,000 the British Admiralty charts of the Maldives cover 3m (10ft) of paper, while the capital island of Malé warrants a mere 6mm (0.23in) speck – and that's after land reclamation has more than doubled its size.

However diminutive Malé may be, there is something strangely compelling and larger-than-life about glimpsing its gold-domed mosque and tight grid of streets as your plane banks above the island in preparation for landing. At first glance, it resembles a fragment of a much larger modern city that has somehow detached itself and floated into the middle of an ocean. Malé has no coral sand beaches or swaying palms. Its lagoon has been concreted over to add precious land to its tenuous 2km^2 (0.8sq.miles), and its coast is piled with surreal-looking concrete blocks, called tetrapods, to dissipate storm-driven waves. Welcome to the capital of Paradise!

Incongruous as Malé may seem after all those evenings you've spent perusing glossy holiday brochures, remember that the Republic of Maldives is a thriving, independent nation with industry, commerce, government and all the other trappings of the 'real world' – some of its buildings rise to as high as 12 storeys. Malé has a population of around 75,000. This oceanic mini-metropolis is well worth an hour or two of exploring on foot, particularly around the fish and produce markets where tuna, coconuts and bananas are piled high.

The Maldives have long been an important maritime trading post. Egyptians, Romans and Mesopotamians may have called by from as early as 2000BC. For centuries the archipelago was known as the 'Money Isles' because it supplied huge quantities of cowry shells – once an important international currency.

It was, however, in AD1153 that Arabs made the biggest impression on the islands' history by converting the Maldivian people to Islam. Legend has it that Rannamaari – a sea jinni – demanded the sacrifice of virgin girls in Malé. A North African Arab, Abu Al Barakat, who was visiting the island, sacrificed himself in place of a girl and used the Koran – the Islamic holy book – to drive away the demon. The king at the time was so impressed by what the Arab had done that the Maldivian people converted to Islam. Barakat became the first of a series of 84 Maldivian sultans.

Right *A short walk to paradise. Once you've arrived at your resort island there is usually a plethora of watersports available, from sailing to scuba diving.*

Right *Each of the Maldives' 1192 islands is composed of coral sand that has built up inside a shallow coral reef lagoon, with lush green palms packed on a patch of land.*

Nowadays, 202 islands (17 per cent of the total) are permanently inhabited. A few fishing villages, like Himmafushi and Dhagathi, can be visited on day trips, but the vast majority of tourists are accommodated on separate, otherwise uninhabited resort islands. Kurumba, the Maldives' first resort, opened on Vihamana Fushi in 1972. There are now around 90 others – each one a self-contained life-support capsule with its own desalination plant, waste disposal system and a host of other refinements that your average desert island castaway could only dream of.

Reaching your resort island is all part of the adventure of a trip to the Maldives. From the 'airport island' of Hulhule (adjacent to Malé) seaplanes and speedboats provide the quickest transfers, but for something more traditional (albeit slower) nothing beats a dhoni (traditional boat). From taxi and freighter to fishing boat and fuel tanker, these ubiquitous and adaptable vessels have been plying the Maldives for centuries, their distinctive scimitar-like prows cleaving the waters.

From the air, the Maldives' reefs and lagoons paint the sea with vivid swirls of turquoise and jade, but at sea level any evidence of the vast archipelago can be difficult to discern. No land in the Maldives rises more than 2.5m (8ft) above sea level, which means that all but the nearest islands are hidden beyond the horizon. As your dhoni putters along, however, distant islands gradually appear as sandy whiskers topped with palms.

Stepping ashore it's impossible not to feel a slight tingle of excitement at the prospect of being 'marooned' on a remote tropical island. A chilled cocktail is pressed into your hand as you're shown to a comfortable beachfront chalet, open to the cooling ocean breezes. Nevertheless, you can't escape the fact that this is an island so small you can probably walk its entire perimeter in 20 minutes. Sooner or later you will need to make a bid for freedom — and that means unpacking your mask and snorkel.

A short swim from the beach and you're transported to another world. In complete contrast to life above the waves (where only a few species of plants and animals have colonized these oceanic isles), the Maldives' coral reefs are a treasure store of biodiversity. No less than 700 varieties of fish, 200 types of coral and literally tens of thousands of different sponges, worms, clams, crabs, starfish and other invertebrates inhabit these 'rainforests of the seas'. There is nowhere in the oceans more diverse, prolific or beautiful.

The fact that the sea temperature in the Maldives remains at a fairly constant 27°C (81°F) year-round is an added incentive to linger as you explore this remarkable seascape. Take your time during a snorkel from lagoon shallows to reef edge and you will witness all kinds of drama — from stingrays gliding beneath you on undulating 'wings' to shoals of parrotfish, a hundred strong, swooping and flitting through groves of coral. Take a breath and free-dive a few metres down to peer into caves where writhing shoals of squirrelfish and cardinal fish await twilight before emerging, and look out for cleaner wrasse, tiny blue-and-white streaked fish, performing dental valets on groupers and angelfish.

Against this dynamic and dazzling background, there are several dive sites in the Maldives that have risen to world-class status. Manta Point on North Malé Atoll, for example, attracts large numbers of manta ray during the southwest monsoon season (May–November). At Embudhu Kandu on South Malé Atoll, a 2km (1.2-mile) channel is the setting for an exhilarating drift dive where

Left *Getting around the islands of the Maldives you have a choice of speedboat, seaplane, helicopter or the traditional dhoni.*
Opposite top *Tourist resorts in the Maldives have idyllic settings, including the one perched on stilts above a shallow, turquoise lagoon.*
Opposite *A scuba diver watches a procession of bannerfish on a coral reef in the Maldives.*

ocean currents sweep you through a realm of grey reef sharks, eagle rays and other large pelagic species. There are also exciting wreck dives in the Maldives, like the British Loyalty that was torpedoed at Addu Atoll in 1944.

To sample far-flung options, diving enthusiasts can join live-aboard cruises. There are also plenty of dive schools at resorts throughout the archipelago for those who want to progress from snorkelling to scuba diving.

However, the Maldives is not simply about goggling at life underwater. Whale-watching safaris operate in deeper water around the atolls between February and May. Species sighted include beaked, blue, Bryde's and sperm whales, as well as bottlenose, Risso's and spinner dolphins.

Surfing, which is popular in the Maldives from March to November, was pioneered by Tony Hussein, who was shipwrecked in the islands during the early 1970s. Then there are more traditional water sports like fishing, sailing and windsurfing.

Whatever lures you to this remote chain of coral islands, however, try not to leave it for too long before visiting. If predictions of global warming and the result-ant rise in sea level are correct, the Maldives could be one of the first nations on earth to be severely affected. An average sea-level rise of just 10mm (0.4in) per year would be enough to submerge the entire country within one or two centuries. Tragically, paradise found could quite literally become paradise lost.

Mauritius

FIONA MCINTOSH

With beautiful beaches, translucent blue water and unbelievable sunsets, Mauritius will meet your expectations of a tropical island paradise. Whether you're a film star hiding away in an ultra-exclusive resort or are on a modest budget, you'll be treated like a honeymooner. Mauritians take hospitality seriously and pride themselves on superb, friendly service, top-class facilities and gourmet cuisine. You could easily spend your entire holiday being pampered, and never feel the urge to leave the manicured grounds. However, to do so would be a travesty, for the island has a huge variety of cultural and natural attractions. Take some time out from the beach to admire the distinctive architecture of the plantation houses, the colourful festivals, walks in the indigenous tropical forests, island sanctuaries and nature reserves.

Mauritius, 1865km² (730sq.miles) in size, sits just north of the Tropic of Capricorn, 800km (500 miles) east of Madagascar, on the trade route between

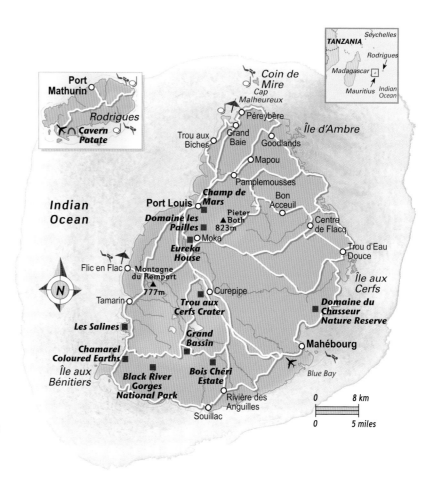

Europe and the East Indies. The volcanic origins of the island are evident in the towering peaks and in some of the island's major tourist attractions, such as the Chamarel Coloured Earths and the Trou aux Cerfs crater. The coral coast, lapped by the warm waters of the Indian Ocean, teems with marine life.

The mix of races reflects Mauritius' development. People of different hues, religions and cultures coexist happily, and this diversity adds to the island's allure. Busy Chinese traders ply their wares next to the country's largest mosque, while on race day the traditional temples around the Champ de Mars horseracing track become impromptu ice cream and snack stalls. French and English are widely spoken, and the variety of cuisine is a gourmet's delight.

Behind the current paradise is a dark and interesting history. The Dutch occupied the island in 1598, naming it Mauritius after the son of William of Orange, Prince Maurice. For the next 100 years they tried to establish a colony, bringing in slaves from Madagascar and prisoners from the East Indies to do the work, and importing sugar cane and animals to boost the food stocks. However, it all came to nothing as drought, cyclones and piracy drove them away.

The French arrived in Mauritius in 1715, and soon the newly named Île de France began to flourish under the dynamic leadership of Mahé de Labourdonnais. Everywhere you go in Mauritius you will come across the name of the island's favourite son who transformed the economy. Despite his good efforts, the colony went into decline at the end of the century. During the Napoleonic Wars, Mauritius became a contested asset between the French and British, and although the French gained a surprise victory at the Battle of Grand Port in 1810 (the only French naval victory during Napoleon's rule), the British gained sovereignty in 1814, remaining until Seewoosagur Ramgoolam (later Sir) was appointed the country's first prime minister following independence in 1968.

Mauritius has two seasons: a hot, wet season from December to April and a cooler, drier season from May to November. Cyclones and heavy rains can occur from January to March, but the climate is warm and pleasant year-round. As you fly in, your impression is of jagged peaks jutting out of the lush, flat plain below. The blue-green of the ocean and the natural aquarium of Blue Bay, almost on the flight path, immediately draw your eye.

The waters are shallow and clear, with sand extending to the encircling reef and offshore islets – some unusual adventures take advantage of this. The adrenaline pumps as you listen to the pre-dive briefing on how to bring the Blue Submarine to the surface, should your captain be indisposed, and the feeling of descending into the deep in a real submarine is surreal, like being in a James Bond movie. Equally bizarre is an undersea walk. Sporting a heavy diving bell helmet you meander along the seabed somewhat like a moonwalker, admiring the reef and colourful tropical fish.

Most resorts have their own private beach and water-skiers, yachtsmen and parasailors buzz up and down the shores. Kite-boarding is popular – the water is warm, the winds fairly predictable and the instruction top-notch. If you visit the north coast, or Cap Malheureux, you will see the sky dotted with the colourful canopies of the daredevil enthusiasts.

In the capital, Port Louis, the waterfront developments are a major attraction, with the al fresco restaurants and quayside walks complementing the country's biggest shopping complex. The sense of calm, and the interactive displays of the Blue Penny museum contrast dramatically with the somewhat eclectic exhibits found in

Right *A picturesque view of the ocean from a point near Cap Malheureux, showing the island of Coin de Mire in the distance.*

Opposite *Flic-en-Flac is a west coast beach lined by palm trees and dotted with thatch 'umbrellas' to provide shade for visitors to this stunning location.*

most of the city's other museums. All have charm, with the stuffed dodo in the unusual collection at the National History Museum being one of the most interesting.

Port Louis is frenetic and noisy, but you can easily spend a few hours wandering around admiring the temples and different ethnic quarters. The highlight is the crowded Central Market. As you wander past the fresh vegetable and flower displays, pungent fish and meat markets and colourful souvenir stalls, opportunist traders deliver their pitch in a number of tongues. Seek out the *tisane* (herbal remedy) stalls and you'll find a cure for any ailment you could imagine, from cellulite to asthma as well as some, apparently, powerful aphrodisiacs.

The horseshoe of dramatic peaks around the capital offers good hiking, while rock climbers can try their luck on Pieter Both, a curious-shaped mountain with a precariously balanced boulder on top, like a head with a cloak forming the flanks. It's named after the admiral and Governor of the Dutch East Indies, who went down with his ship, the *Banda*, in a tropical cyclone in 1615.

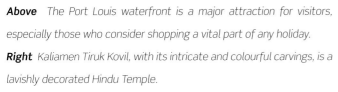

Above *The Port Louis waterfront is a major attraction for visitors, especially those who consider shopping a vital part of any holiday.*

Right *Kaliamen Tiruk Kovil, with its intricate and colourful carvings, is a lavishly decorated Hindu Temple.*

Opposite left *At the spice market, you can get a herbal remedy for anything from cellulite to arthritis to powerful aphrodisiacs.*

The large estate of Domaine les Pailles, just outside Port Louis, has an old-fashioned charm, some superb restaurants and a casino. Tours in a gleaming, black horse-drawn carriage or a miniature train, include a reconstructed sugar mill, a rum distillery and a spice garden.

Dubbed Mauritius' Cote d'Azur, the big, sheltered crescent of Grand Baie, with its myriad restaurants, shops and galleries, has a buzz felt nowhere else on the island. Sunset Boulevard, a cluster of chic boutiques, bars and tour agencies hums by day, and at night the town comes alive with a glittering array of gaudy Chinese restaurants, pubs and clubs.

The small resort of Péreybère is popular with snorkellers, swimmers and families who enjoy trips on the glass-bottomed boats. Graceful filaos trees line the beach,

providing shade for locals and tourists alike as they enjoy dhall purri from street and motorbike vendors.

The top spot to enjoy Mauritius' national dance, the hip swaying, sensual *séga* is on the beach at Trou aux Biches. As the sun sets, fires are lit and the *séga* troupe arrives by dhow – the elegant women dressed in tight bodices and flowing skirts and their dark-skinned partners in short breeches and open-neck shirts dance to the beat of the ravan, a goatskin tambourine.

Other fun things to do from Grand Baie are trips on the luxury schooner, the *Isla Mauritia*, and catamaran trips to the picturesque north coast islands. The distinctive wedge-shaped Coin de Mire, home to many of the islands best dive sites, including the wreck of the *Jabeeda* and wonderful coral gardens, dominates the horizon and

lunch is served off Îlot Gabriel, a tiny, flat sandbank where you can cool down and snorkel in the shallows.

The Botanical Gardens at Pamplemousses are one of the highlights of a trip to the island. Originally part of the home of the Mahé de Labourdonnais, the gardens are a tranquil place to stroll or picnic and admire the varied and colourful floral specimens. Key exhibits include the royal palms of Poivre Avenue, the lotus pond and the waterlily pond, with its vast leaves like upturned tart dishes. They look so solid and inviting that it is tempting to use them as stepping stones.

At l'Aventure du Sucre (Sugar World), next door, an old sugar mill has been transformed into a modern, stimulating museum, which records the history of sugar – the mainstay of the Mauritian economy for many years, and the industry's role in shaping the landscape and people. The spacious, well-laid out exhibition is rivalled only by the Blue Penny Museum in the Caudan Waterfront of Port Louis.

Many of the island's old colonial houses have been well preserved and give a fascinating insight into the Creole culture. Typical of the style is the magnificent mansion of Eureka, near Moka, with its 109 doors, and a shaded veranda on which you can enjoy tea or a light meal. For a complete tea experience, head for Bois Chéri Estate. The tour culminates in a tasting at a beautifully located chalet overlooking the plantation and escarpment.

Curepipe and its suburbs are known for model-ship workshops, jewellery, clothing and gemstone boutiques, and a visit to the circular Trou aux Cerfs crater, from where you can look out over almost the whole island, is a must.

One of the most incredible spectacles, the festival of Maha Shivaratri, takes place at Grand Bassin further south

Top left Why the earths of Chamarel are the colours they are is open to debate; what is not disputed is their beauty.
Left The waterlilies afloat on the pond in the Botanical Gardens at Pamplemousses look like gigantic pie dishes.
Opposite The walk along the vista of sea-carved cliffs and caves between Pointe Coton and Trou d'Argent on the island of Rodrigues is not to be missed.

on the central plateau. In late February/early March, devout Hindus adorned in bright saris and flowing white robes flock from all over the country on their annual pilgrimage to pay homage to Lord Shiva. Once at the lake, *puja* ceremonies take place, with sacrifices and prayers offered up to the gods – flowers and fruits peppered with burning incense sticks are floated on the lake.

The calm conditions, extensive white sand beach and proximity of the edge of the reef make Flic en Flac, on the west coast, a popular holiday resort and an ideal base for scuba diving. The Hindu Kali temple nearby is a good place to experience the end-of-year fire-walking ceremonies – Teemeedee. A great fire is lit, sacrifices are made and the coals are beaten and blessed by brightly robed priests before the initiates – many of whom are in a trance after a week of fasting and preparation – step over the glowing embers.

In Tamarin, slightly further south, waves roll into the bay through a natural break in the reef, and surfers and kayakers go out to play among the dolphins. The view of the mountains from the bay is one of the best on the island. In summer, the river is lined with scarlet-blossomed trees and the dramatic triangular profile of the Rempart mountain – the Matterhorn of Mauritius – casts its reflection in the river. A short drive through Les Salines – the only surviving examples of the salt marshes introduced by Labourdonnais – is the premier big-game fishing resort of Black River, which hosts the annual Marlin World Cup competition every December. The wild south coast is dramatic. Waves crash against the high, black cliffs sending sprays of seawater through spouts and fissures and eroding picturesque sea arches. This is a place to lose yourself, to walk with the wind in your hair and admire the magnificence of nature.

One of Mauritius's best-kept secrets is the tiny dependency of Rodrigues, 560km (350 miles) to the northeast. Protected by an encircling coral reef and wide lagoon, the island boasts dramatic sea cliffs, deserted beaches and a necklace of offshore islets. Outside the town of Port Mathurin, with its quaint street market, there is little development except for a couple of small, intimate resorts built in the classic Creole style. Rodrigues is drier than the main island, the people are a darker hue and fishing or harvesting of octopus are the means of subsistence. The diving and snorkelling are superb, and there are boat trips over the vast, turquoise lagoon to the pristine island sanctuaries of Île Cocos and Île aux Sables, where you'll see rare terns and the Rodriguan fody. Other attractions include the Cavern Patate, a labyrinth of limestone caves, and the annual Fish Festival in the first week of March, but it's the pace of life and the openness of the smiling, hardworking people that makes this place special.

Mauritius is full of surprises, and its attractions are far greater than the clichéd image of paradise that is often portrayed. It's a safe place to soak up the reviving sun and the fragrance of tropical flowers; to enjoy the sound of the sea and the rare mix of exotic cultures. Whether you go for a family, romantic or active holiday, it's a place that you'll leave with fond memories and the intention to return.

Réunion

FIONA McINTOSH

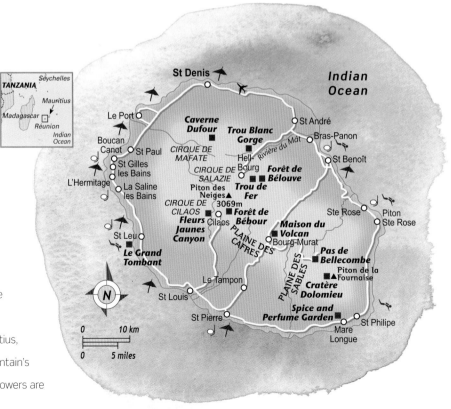

Réunion holds many of the typical attractions of a tropical island, but additionally, its unique mountainous topography gives it a wild edge and provides the visitor with incredible opportunities for exploration. The island is dominated by an ancient volcano, Piton des Neiges, surrounded by three, deep, concave craters: the cirques of Mafate, Cilaos and Salazie. These sheer-sided valleys, initially the product of cataclysmic volcanic activity, have been eroded by rivers to form razor-sharp ridges, deep gorges and boulder-strewn ravines which run from the central mountains to the coast. The Piton de la Fournaise volcano in the east is one of the most active in the world.

In many ways Réunion is similar to its better-known neighbour, Mauritius, which lies 180km (112 miles) to the northeast. Lush forests clothe the mountain's flanks, spices and sugar cane are widely cultivated, and tropical fruits and flowers are in abundance. Sun-worshippers play on the golden beaches, water sports are popular, and there's great diving on the coral reef. But Réunion offers much more than just the hedonistic pleasures of sun, sand and sea. The island, with its incredible array of adventures in a concentrated area, is ideal for those who seek an active holiday. You can be up on the summit of Piton des Neiges at sunrise, enjoy a challenging mountain-bike descent and watch sunset on the beach. And, for the less energetic, there are gentle walks in the forest, interesting museums, architecture and crafts, plus superb cuisine to enjoy.

Réunion is 2512km² (985sq.miles) in size, with a circumference of 207km (129 miles). The island is an overseas department of France and, despite the 10,000km (6214 miles) that separate it from the mother country, it is still very French. Réunion's historical development is similar to that of Mauritius, and its population mix is the result of influxes of slaves and indentured labourers during the sugar and spice heydays.

There are two seasons: a cool dry season from April to September and a hot, wet, cyclonic season from October to March. But the high mountains mean that the weather is always unpredictable, and on most days the interior is shrouded with cloud by lunchtime.

The best way to orientate yourself is via a helicopter flip. As you climb up the steep, vegetated slopes, the volcanic origins of the island are evident. Vast basalt walls mark the extent of the cirques, and dramatic black cliffs and promontories punctuate the coastline. The chopper skims the ridges before plunging into the deep, circular valley of Trou de Fer, a wonderland of waterfalls and narrow gorges inaccessible by land. You pass over the luxuriant, indigenous forests of Bébour-Bélouve and soar over the more gentle slopes of Plaine des Cafres till you aresuddenly over the barren slopes and cones of Piton de la Fournaise. Peering into these old craters is incredible, and you'll see evidence of the continuing activity in the steaming vents and occasional red-hot lava seams.

The international airport is close to the capital, St Denis, a lively town of bistros, restaurants and clubs, particularly around the old harbour district of the Barachois. This seaside park, with its palms and pavement cafés, is very popular with local families, petanque (bowls) players and tourists alike. The bustling market, tranquil

Jardin de l'Etat, Léon Dierx museum – home to the most famous collection of art in the Indian Ocean – and the impressive, if somewhat decaying, Creole and colonial buildings of the Rue de Paris are a short stroll away.

The west of the island is warm and dry. At St Gilles, the most important tourist resort, the pretty harbour is packed with eateries, bars and shops. The extensive beach of Roches Noires attracts the young and trendy; while around the quayside fresh seafood restaurants are interspersed with diving and fishing centres, and a modern, informative aquarium.

The neighbouring L'Hermitage and La Saline les Bains are also popular, particularly with families; while Boucan Canot has a cluster of superb hotels, an exquisite beach, great snorkelling and an excellent wave.

The Riviera starts at St Paul, famous for its colourful seafront, weekend market and the Cimetière Marin. Among the colourful characters resting here are the notorious pirate, Le Buse (the buzzard) who was hanged in St Paul in 1730, the poet Leconte de Lisle, and the unfortunate Eraste Feuillet. A man of exaggerated honour, Feuillet offered up his own pistol when his duelling opponent's failed. His epitaph *victime de sa générosité* needs no translation.

Right *Activity at the tiny harbour in St Gilles les Bains starts to die down as night-time approaches.*

Opposite *A group of hikers enjoys the captivating sunrise on Piton des Neiges, the highest point on the island of Reunion.*

St Leu is one of the world's top surfing and paragliding spots. A tandem paragliding flight gives an incredible bird's-eye view of the surrounding coastline. The island's top scuba diving site, the famous wall, Le Grand Tombant, is accessed from the tiny harbour. The Stella Matutina Museum, a former sugar factory, provides a good insight into the history of the island.

The wild south, with its rocky cliffs and wild seas, is the centre for many of the spices and essential oils. St Pierre, its biggest centre, is a popular yachting harbour and its cemetery, mosque and colourful Tamil temples are worth visiting. The nearby forest of Mare Longue, has botanical trails, while the Spice and Perfume Garden is a gem, with guided tours of the three-acre reserve and its 1500 species.

Despite the allure of the coast, most visitors head for the hills, embarking on well-marked day trails or trekking into the remoter regions of the cirques. Few roads penetrate the interior, but there are 2000km (1243 miles) of designated hiking routes. Long-distance trails circumnavigate the cirques and traverse the island, taking in the mountains and the volcano. The Cirque de Mafate is the wildest and most pristine region and the villages there, inaccessible by car, have a true alpine character. A series of conveniently located and extremely comfortable *gîtes* – mountain huts complete with beds and hot showers – make hiking quite luxurious.

Left *For the brave at heart, undertake a tandem paragliding flight to experience Réunion's Riviera from a different perspective.*

Below *Visitors can enjoy a guided tour of the lush green Spice and Perfume Garden in the southeast of Réunion.*

Opposite *Canyoning down Fleurs Jaunes may appeal to tourists who prefer spending their time engaged in adventurous activities.*

A drive to the picturesque town of Cilaos, up a giddying succession of switchbacks and hairpin bends, is an adventure in itself. The town, with its traditional architecture and quaint restaurants, is an excellent base for mountain sports. An ascent of Piton des Neiges, 3069m (1007ft), is possible for the average hiker but is a steep, sustained climb. A round trip is feasible in a day, but it's more enjoyable to overnight at the Caverne Dufour hut and watch the sunrise. While mountain biking – known locally as *vélo tout-terrain* (VTT) – canyoning down the precipitous falls of the Fleurs Jaunes valley and hiking are popular, Cilaos is best known for its thermal baths – the only ones in the Indian Ocean – where you can enjoy a spa treatment, shiatsu or hydromassage. Local wine tasting is offered at the small co-operative.

Trade winds bring heavy rain to the east of the island, and the forests are dense and lush. Hell-Bourg, the major village in the Salazie cirque, sits in a beautiful amphitheatre. The drive along the Rivière du Mât gorge is charming, taking you past tumbling waterfalls and traditional wooden houses, while the valley offers great hiking and some exciting canyoning in the Trou Blanc gorge. Bras-Panon, at the coastal end of the gorge, is the island's vanilla capital, and vanilla tours are offered here and at nearby St André. The large Indian community makes St André a good place to watch the Tamil fire-walking ceremonies in December to January, or catch the Chinese street dragon dance marking the start of the Chinese New Year.

The active volcano of Piton de la Fournaise is one of Réunion's biggest attractions. If you just want the view you can drive – or ride a horse – across the desolate, reddish-brown Plaine des Sables (plain of sand) to Pas de Bellecombe on the crater rim. But to really appreciate the caldera and various cones, start early and make the steep hike down into the main crater and the still active Cratère Dolomieu. The excellent Maison du Volcan in Bourg-Murat has in-depth displays, recordings and footage of volcanic activity.

Whether you come for gastronomy, culture or adventure, Réunion will not disappoint. The island offers a wealth of experiences that few countries, never mind islands, can match. Its treasures have remained hidden from most of the world for too long; now the secret is out.

Zanzibar

GRAHAM MERCER

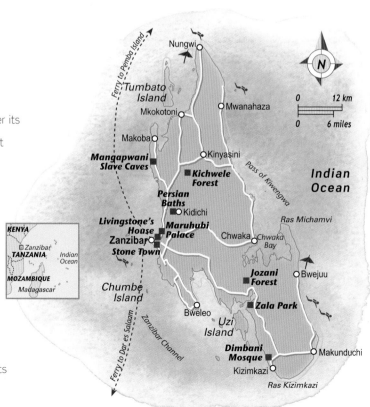

ake a chunk of coral 85km (53 miles) long and 20km (12 miles) wide, cover its western sector with a topsoil so rich that a walking stick poked into it will burst into leaf, spread white coral sand along its shoreline, especially the northern and eastern coasts, and set the whole thing down in a typically blue tropical sea, 40km (25 miles) off one of the word's most interesting countries. Then give it a name beginning with 'Z' and you've created a cliché. Pity Zanzibar has no mountains; even its hills look as if the earth is just taking a deep breath – but you can't have everything.

'Magical', Zanzibar most certainly is. Black and white magic is practised in places, especially on the island of Pemba, which together with Unguja – Zanzibar Island as it is known to most of us – and many islets make up the Zanzibar archipelago. Would-be witchdoctors from as far afield as Haiti are said to come to Pemba to learn their trade. And while we're on the subject of Zanzibar-as-a-whole, as opposed to Unguja, let's quickly define its political status.

After a bloody revolution in 1964, it was joined to newly independent Tanganyika to form the United Republic of Tanzania. Not the happiest of marriages, though the archipelago gets on with life and with its mainland partner.

The problem with Zanzibar is that it doesn't always fit the 'exotic' and 'romantic' templates that advertising tries to impose on it. Its history (introduced from abroad), which is undeniably fascinating and one of Zanzibar's major attractions, was certainly exotic in the true meaning of the word, for much of the islands' past involved outsiders. They were settled during the ninth or 10th centuries by Persian and Arab merchants who arrived in dhows and took African wives, resulting in the so-called Swahili civilization. Some lived in surprising opulence, but their little city-states fought like feral cats and their economies were underpinned by slavery.

'Exotic' can also mean 'barbarous'. And, although this definition is rarely used nowadays, it might be appropriate with regard to the exotic Portuguese who arrived in 1498, bringing some pretty brutal Western enlightenment. Astonished to find an advanced Islamic civilization (and coveting its gold), they asserted their bruised sense of Western superiority by attacking the people of the islands. Zanzibar got off relatively lightly, but the locals got the message. They co-operated with the Portuguese for two centuries until the Europeans were replaced by the Omanis.

In 1832, the man who first put Zanzibar on the map, Said, Sultan of Oman, took a shine to Zanzibar and moved house to Unguja — the first of its Omani ruling dynasty. He had 'acquired' the throne by shoving a dagger into the stomach of his father's cousin, which was par for the course in 18th-century Oman, but fairly 'exotic' (in its barbaric sense) nevertheless. Said, in all fairness, was a most unusual, enterprising man in more acceptable ways, and lived to be called, with much justification, 'Said the Great'.

He transformed Zanzibar into a 19th-century Dubai, partly through cloves and coconuts, partly through slaves and ivory. Three-quarters of Zanzibar's population in the mid-19th century were slaves; countless others were shipped off to the Gulf and elsewhere. The younger, prettier females wound up in the harems of the sultans or those of the Arab and Swahili merchant princes, such as slave-and-ivory trader Tippu Tip, guarded by crudely castrated eunuchs. You can't get more 'exotic' than that.

The sultans' huge families lived in palaces, many situated by the sea. Mtoni had gardens where peacocks, flamingoes and antelopes wandered among clouds of jasmine, oleander and frangipani, and from which, at times, Princess Salme — daughter of Said — looked out over waters scattered with dhows, manned by crews

straight from *Sinbad the Sailor*. All – if you weren't a slave or sailor – very 'romantic'.

The main palace complexes in the Stone Town, flanked by the mansions of the sultan's advisors and friends, dominated a waterfront which quickly became one of the world's most historical and political, its southeastern sector lined with consulates. Behind the waterfront with its secrets and intrigues, a maze of narrow alleys, lined by high, square Arab houses, plain without but lavishly furnished within, and Indian bazaars, buzzing with vitality (and flies), made up the town's multicultural matrix. Then, as now, the bazaars were crammed with tiny, open-fronted dukas, selling anything from 'Zanzibar' chests to clocks and coriander.

Above the dukas, fretworked wooden balconies projected from walls made interesting by shuttered windows and fanlights of multicoloured glass, proclaim the Gujerati origins of the shopkeepers. But despite its cosmopolitan nature, the Stone Town was a Muscat-in-miniature; its palaces and mansions built around beautifully carved 'Zanzibar' doors, and embellished by saracenic arches, recessed windows and castellated parapets. Even the backstreets echo to the sound of the

Right *What is most likely to remind any visitor of their trip to Stone Town is its famous carved doors: the Zanzibar Doors.*

Opposite *One of the world's most historical waterfronts — a dhow off Shangani Point, Zanzibar island.*

azan from the mosques, and to the cries of Omani-style coffee boys, with their conical brass pots, and, in the late afternoon, the cry of slave dealers as they herd their cattle to the market.

There are smells also, at least one of them pleasant; the aroma of cloves is everywhere. The coconut groves to the north of the Stone Town yield spices and fruits with names that bewitch the imagination, or at least the taste buds. One of them, ground nutmeg, is mixed by Zanzibari men into their loved one's porridge, 'to make them say' and, presumably do, 'nice things'.

Before we are overpowered by exotic smells and the romance of veiled women steeped in *oud* and libidinous with powdered nutmeg, let's try to achieve a more balanced perspective by turning to the celebrated 19th-century explorers who passed through Zanzibar. The savagely brilliant Richard Burton, not known for his PR skills, knew a thing or two about romance (one kind at least), having translated the *Arabian Nights, Perfumed Garden* and *Kama Sutra*. He likened the faces of Zanzibari women (admittedly its 'ladies of the night') to those of 'skinned apes'. Livingstone, presumably less well-acquainted with eastern brothels, directed his own cutting comments at the slave trade, but he wasn't fooled by the smell of cloves; he called Unguja 'Stinkibar'. Henry Morton Stanley merely talks of the islands' 'bouquet from windward, comprised of cloves and copra, sweat and sewage'. And Joseph Thomson talks of Zanzibar's 'glamour and fascination' being 'only too often dispelled by the rude facts of experience'.

Don't cancel your bookings. Not because things have changed, but because in many ways they haven't. And if the explorers, sultans, slaves and great ocean-going dhows have gone, you can, with a little imagination and reading, reinvent them. And you should, as much of Zanzibar's allure is in its history. So don't be put off. Zanzibar is exotic – if you come from somewhere else – and romantic. In any case, if you want squeaky clean streets and no bad smells, rats, drug addicts or graffiti, you can go to Berne. But if you want to experience Arabia, India and Africa, and history all in one, Zanzibar has it. With spices, beautiful beaches and coral gardens, excellent diving and game fishing thrown in.

Don't neglect the Stone Town. And don't just edge through the popular bazaars half expecting to be mugged. Get involved and get lost – literally. Unless you're very unlucky or foolish, the worst that will happen is that you'll be irritated by the would-be guides. If you're a bit nervous, go in a group or with a guide recommended by your hotel. But go. And don't expect a museum, though you'll find the 19th century if you look for it, and much to interest you in the 21st. See all the obvious places, the Old Dispensary, the former sultan's palace, the 'House of Wonders', the Old Fort and the Cathedral Church of Christ on the site of the old slave market. If you enjoy architecture, see John Sinclair's Peace Museum and the law courts, the Old Post Office and the Bharmal Building. But wander along the waterfront, through the bazaars and into Stone Town's nooks and crannies. Pop into the old dhow harbour, if only to prove that dhows are not quite so romantic close up.

In the late afternoon, stroll around Shangani to see the old British consulate where several famous explorers stayed before leaving to seek the source of the Nile, or a grave in Westminster Abbey. Livingstone, who ironically wanted to be buried in an African forest, found the latter; his shrivelled remains once lay here. Next door is the Tembo Hotel, once the American consulate where Stanley stayed, and a short walk away is the house of his old safari partner, the slaver Tippu Tip, with its fine door and atmospheric ambience. Before sunset have a 'sundowner' drink on the terrace of the nearby Africa House Hotel or at Serena, or opt for a soft drink on the verandah of the nonalcoholic Tembo. After dark, go to the street-food stalls at Forodhani, between the 'House of Wonders' and the sea. Dishes include kingfish, king prawns or lobster fresh from the sea. Get stuck in, don't just gawp. And make sure you try the delightfully rubbery 'Zanzibar bread'.

Out of town, take a 'spice' tour, which includes a visit to the ruins of Sultan Barghash's harem at Maruhubi and

Above *Award-winning Chumbe Island Lodge, is a delightful location for naturalists and snorkellers.*

Opposite *It is common to see fleets of tiny boats, called dhows, bobbing on the shallow waters of Zanzibar.*

perhaps the Persian baths at Kidichi, built by Sultan Said for one of his wives, Sherehezade. Stop off briefly at Livingstone's House on the way. But choose a tour that provides lunch cooked by the ladies of one of the villages and eaten under an open *banda* (hut), sitting on the floor as even the sultans did. The food is simple but the spices would make just about anything edible.

Take a boat to one of the islets, and go swimming or have a picnic. Spend a night or two on Chumbe Island, which has won awards for its coral reefs and conservation. Day trips to Chumbe can be arranged at the Protea Mbweni Ruins Hotel across the channel, known for its lovely botanical gardens and interesting late 19th-century ruins. Then there is swimming with the dolphins down south at Kizimkazi. Don't expect the Barrier Reef; the Zanzibar dolphins are more often chased around the bay when tourists leap out and alarm them. But it's worth going to see the indige-nous Zanzibar Red Monkeys in Jozani Forest en route, and the little 12th-century mosque in Kizimkazi village, where the old caretaker will show you around.

Which brings us to the beaches, dazzling white coral strands lined by palms and shelving into seas that for most of the year look as if a fleet of great dhows, loaded with aquamarine, sapphires, tanzanite, turquoise and lapis lazuli had sunk in some ancient storm and spilled their cargoes into the clear water. And if all this sounds like advertising hype, so be it; that's how it is.

Among Unguja's best beaches are Nungwi in the north and Bwejuu in the east, but there are many others. And in Pemba, Funda Lagoon and Misali Island, with its superb coral reefs and if you believe the legend, Captain Kidd's buried treasure, plus many other fine beaches and coves, though getting to some might be an adventure.

But adventure is what Zanzibar is all about, whether it's a 'Hey, do you think we should really be doing this?' experience, which might apply in parts of Pemba or among the submarine reefs, or something more 'house slippers by the hearth', such as losing yourself temporarily in the Stone Town or risking being brained by a falling coconut as you lie in your hammock in Nungwi. Chances are you'll survive, and chances are you'll get to understand why Sultan Said moved house from Muscat; he recognized the exotic and the romantic when he saw them.

Above *Bali, deemed by many to be the most beautiful island on earth, is one of many jewels of the ocean that draw us to the islands of the Pacific.*

Asia and the Pacific

Bali

ROWLAND MEAD

The island of Bali is often characterized as the 'the last paradise on earth', a description based on factors such as its magnificent volcanic scenery, its luxuriant vegetation and its gentle, artistic people. This image took a severe dent on October 12, 2002, when a terrorist's bomb ripped into the heart of a nightclub in the resort of Kuta, killing 202 people, tourists and locals alike. Bali's 10/12 became as infamous as America's 9/11 and will be a burden that the island will struggle to throw off for years to come.

Bali is one of a string of islands making up the Indonesian archipelago, which stretches for 5000km (3106 miles) from Malaysia to Australia. The island has an area of just 5632km² (2174sq.miles) and measures 90km (55 miles) from north to south, and 140km (90 miles) from east to west. Bali is largely volcanic in origin, as it lies over a major subduction zone where

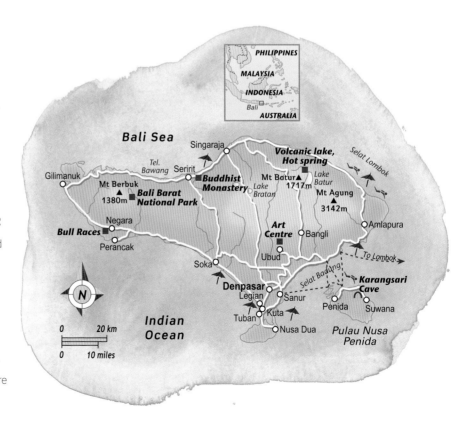

the Indo-Australian plate collides with the rigid Sunda plate, with explosive results. In the north, volcanoes such as Gunung Agung, 3142m (10,308ft), and Gunung Batur, 1717m (5633ft), dominate the landscape, and in the past their fine volcanic ash had provided the rich soils for the prolific crop growing in the south.

Batur had a major eruption in 1926 and the volcano remains active today, with occasional ejections of molten rock and ash. The most recent eruption occurred in 1963 when Gunung Agung was active for six months, causing widespread devastation and the deaths of over 2000 people. It is believed that the Indonesian archipelago once formed a land ridge, but this was converted into a string of islands in the post-glacial rise in sea level. There was, however, always a sea channel between Bali and Lombok, its neighbour to the west. This channel is now known as the Wallace Line – named for a British naturalist – and divides the Asian flora and fauna to the west from the Australian species to the east. Monkeys and tigers, for example, are not found to the east of Bali.

Lying between eight and nine degrees south of the equator, Bali has an equatorial climate, with high temperatures and rain throughout the year; however, there is a distinct cooler, drier season from April to October. The driest parts of the island are in the lowland areas to the south, where coincidentally the best beaches are found. This has led to the development of popular resorts such as Kuta, Sanur and Nusa Dua.

Inland, forests, deep valleys lined with rice terraces and thriving agricultural villages typify the scenery. The wide variety of tropical plants never fails to amaze visitors, and there are flowers everywhere. You will see and smell frangipani, hibiscus, jasmine, bougainvillea, water lilies and a host of orchid varieties, which line the roads, fill gardens and decorate the temple grounds. Flowers bedeck statues, and are offered to the gods in temples. It seems entirely natural that your waitress wears a flower behind her ear.

Bali has a population of just over three million. The main town and administrative centre is the fast-growing Denpasar, with 370,000 inhabitants. The overwhelming

majority of the Balinese are Hindus, but this Hinduism is unique. It is a fusion of mainstream Hinduism with elements of Buddhism and animism. Gods and ancestors are honoured, and there are cyclical holidays celebrating such things as books, crops and musical instruments. Essential in all these rituals is the offering of food and flowers. Religious instruction, although taught in schools, is more often passed on through music and dance. Simplified performances of this theatre are often provided for tourists. As with other Hindu countries, a semi-feudal caste system operates and this pervades all areas of public life, and has even been adapted to tourist occupations so that a hotel manager might be given an honorary position.

It is thought that the first migrants arrived in Bali c2500BC, but it was a further 2000 years before the Hindu religion became influential. The 16th century saw the appearance of the European colonial powers and, in particular, the setting up of the Dutch East India Company. By 1850, the Dutch government was administering Bali, and in the early years of the 20th century it controlled practically all of the Indonesian islands. In the 1920s and 1930s there came the first hint of Bali's potential for tourism as a number of well-known artists and writers took up residence on the island, attracted by its special magic. This had the effect of causing an artistic

Right *The best-known Balinese dance is the Kecak, which has an accompaniment of chanting men, rather than the usual gamelan orchestra.*

Opposite *The 17th-century Ulun Danu temple is located on the shore of Lake Bratan, which occupies a volcanic caldera on the island.*

and cultural revival among the Balinese, with craft activities largely based around the inland town of Ubud.

During World War II, the Japanese invaded Indonesia and occupied Bali from 1942 until 1945. After the war, the Dutch tried to regain Indonesia. In the revolution that followed, the Balinese were pro-Dutch, but an Indonesian republic was then finally recognized as an independent state in 1949, with Bali as one of its provinces. The 1960s were a time of violence and attempted coups throughout Indonesia, which were brought to an end by the emergence of the military leader Suharto who became the President of Indonesia.

The stability that Suharto's government brought provided the ideal conditions for the growth of the tourist industry in Bali. With the development of long-distance air travel, tourism in Bali soared in the 1970s. Backpackers soon discovered Bali and it became part of the 'hippie trail'. By 1977, Bali had some 450,000 visitors and this total had grown to over one million in 1990. From just a few hundred hotel rooms in 1965 there were over 30,000 in 1999.

The lively resort of Kuta is situated on the best beach on the island, attracting surfers, swimmers and sunbathers. Once a 17th-century slave port, Kuta is now an international beach resort pulsating to the noisy rhythm of hedonism. Bars, nightclubs, souvenir shops, restaurants, boutiques and small hotels line the coastal strip and the narrow lanes leading inland. Kuta has now spread to envelop neighbouring Legian to the north and Tuban to the south. Highly popular with young Australians, Kuta is definitely not the place for a quiet holiday. To escape the excesses of Kuta, head for the altogether quieter Sanur. This has a number of mid- and upper-range hotels,

Above left *The popular Sanur beach is protected by a reef and embellished by beautifully coloured traditional outrigger fishing boats.*

Left *Bali's rich volcanic soil and abundant rainfall make it ideal for excellent rice cultivation, especially on the terraced hill slopes.*

Opposite *From the rim of Batur caldera, the stunning view across the waters of Lake Batur to mounts Abang and Agung, is truly amazing.*

whose landscaped grounds lead to a beach stretching for 4km (2.5 miles) and embellished by colourful outriggers and other craft. Water sports are available and there is a lively beach market.

To the south is the purpose-built, up-market resort of Nusa Dua, a complex entered through a road lined with statues and a large split gate (*candi beniar*) festooned with carvings of frogs as guardian figures. Here there are internationally famous five-star hotels, with convention centres, a golf course and the Galleria shopping complex. It is quite possible to stay a fortnight at Nusa Dua and see nothing of the real Bali.

There are plans for the future development of the northern fringe of the island, which has a drier, almost Mediterranean-type climate. The main attraction inland is the small town of Ubud, which is claimed to be the cultural heart and soul of Bali. Artists, writers and anthropologists popularized Ubud in the 1920s and 1930s, which encouraged the rebirth of its artistic traditions. Today it is no longer a quiet backwater, but a lively town full of art and craft shops, boutiques and restaurants, with the unpolluted air full of gamelan music. There are temples and museums to visit, along with the Monkey Forest Sanctuary.

So can Bali's tourist industry survive the terrorist's bomb? The signs are very good, for despite the changes caused by the rapid development of Bali's economy, the influx of people from other Indonesian islands and the strong interests of big business, the essential Bali remains 'the paradise island'. Tourists will definitely not stay away for too long.

Lord Howe Island

PHILIP GAME

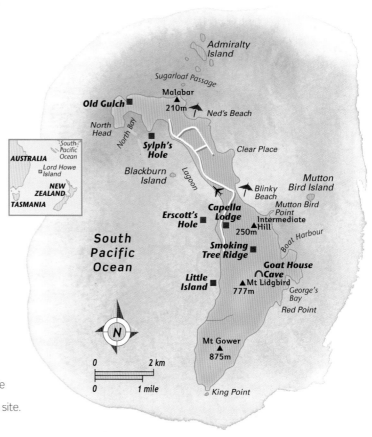

Alone in the Tasman Sea, 700km (420 miles) northeast of Sydney, the sheer-sided twin crags of mounts Lidgbird and Gower have become emblematic of an island retreat which relatively few Australians ever see for themselves. Far from the tropical waters of the Great Barrier Reef yet more costly to reach, Lord Howe Island remains largely the preserve of a discerning few.

At the southern end of this 11km-long (6.8 mile) island, the remnants of an ancient shield volcano, measuring barely 3km (1.86 miles) across, stand the twin massifs, clothed in cloud forests. A lesser peak anchors the island's northern tip. Clinging to their feet is the world's most southerly fringing coral reef, bathed by tropical currents flowing down from the Great Barrier Reef to merge with temperate waters moving west from New Zealand.

Daytime summer temperatures hover around 26°C (80°F), tempered by sea breezes and easing to 16°C (60°F) in winter. The result is an eclectic assemblage of inshore tropical marine life mingling with ocean-going temperate species . Many seabirds breed only on this World Heritage site.

Discovered and named by Lieutenant Ball in the Royal Navy's Supply while sailing from Sydney to Norfolk Island in 1788, Lord Howe Island remained uninhabited for almost another half century. In May that year, Surgeon Arthur Bowes of the *Lady Penrhyn* recorded the astonishing ease with which the island's flightless birds could be taken.

Lord Howe Island's 300 permanent inhabitants descend from a motley bunch of colonial seamen and their New Zealand Maori wives, set ashore by the whaler *Caroline* in 1834. By then, passing ships' crews had decimated the flightless birds; the white gallinule and the white-throated pigeon had disappeared forever.

The Lord Howe Island woodhen remained as a tasty little morsel for colonists well accustomed to game meats, but its numbers were soon decimated.

For a few decades the islanders eked out a living supplying passing whalers, until the whales, too, disappeared. Enter the kentia, a hardy yet attractive palm endemic to the island's volcanic slopes, which for more than a century has adorned living rooms all over the world.

Tourism is now a bigger money-spinner, although the nearest thing to nightlife you'll encounter is a bird dropping out of a tree to fall at your feet. The island is part of the Australian state of New South Wales, although governed by some unique local regulations. Visitor lodgings are capped at about 400 beds and must be pre-booked before arrival.

This is a compact community where all supplies are imported and everyone wears several hats. As for the traffic, two wheels are as common as four, and here nobody bothers with locks. Need a snorkel and flippers? Help yourself and put your money in the box.

From 1947 until the 1970s visitors arrived by flying boats. Now, after two hours of droning over the ocean, the propeller-driven Dash-8 comes to rest on the airstrip carved across the island's centre. The barefoot Kevin Wilson, a genial scion of the dynasty, which has operated the Ocean View tourist lodge for nearly a century, conducts his arriving guests down a road lined with imposing Norfolk Pines, past carefully manicured lawns and fairways, public barbecues and bicycle racks: unmistakable signs of a flourishing tourist trade.

Just over the dunes, the breakers roll in from New Zealand, Land of the Long White Cloud, to dissipate in a lather of spume over the golden sands of Blinky Beach.

Above right *The large fish species, Giant Kingfish, inhabit the waters off Ned's Beach of Lord Howe Island.*

Right *It is quite common to see ducks waddling along the quiet shores of Ned's Beach on the island.*

Opposite *The peaceful and picturesque lagoon is a perfect getaway spot for tourists who want to lie back and watch the boats sailing across the waters.*

Beyond the beach, mounts Lidgbird and Gower sulk under their mantles of cloud. The lower slopes are clothed in mottled green, but then the layered lava flows reach for the clouds. Around March the Providence Petrels arrive, seabirds which nest only on these precipitous cliffs and stage spectacular flying displays.

An emerald ground dove darts out as the track passes through a fern glade; pairs of russet-brown woodhen – once one of the world's most endangered species – browse under the kentias. In the 1970s, barely two dozen breeding pairs of the Lord Howe Island woodhen, *Tricholimnus sylvestrus*, survived on the precipitous flanks of Mt Gower. After many years and much expense, wildlife experts

developed a captive breeding programme, which has been so successful that this flightless rail has regained much of the lowland habitat it enjoyed in the halcyon days before feral cats, pigs and humans intruded.

Returning to civilization, such as it is, the first pit stop is a minor miracle. Capella South Lodge appears on the side of a grassy hill just at the point at which you're more than ready to ease your groin off the bicycle saddle.

Capella's White Gallinule bistro exudes an understated, outdoorsy cool, but the formidable bluffs looming beyond the grazing paddocks remind one of sterner challenges than demolishing a gourmet lunch. Just ahead lies the start of an epic eight-hour scramble up Mt Gower, a refuge for birds and flowering plants which have evolved apart from the rest of the planet.

Be prepared for this loaf of black lava rising nearly 900m (3000ft) out of the water. Visitors don hard hats, the climb is steep before reaching the Low Road, a wide ledge where the forested scree slope meets the lava cliffs.

Here you can stop to catch your breath, while the guide points out some salient features of the kentia palm and its kissing cousin`s.

Once back on the trail, the ledge narrows alarmingly, and if this were the first taste of how to scale Mt Gower, ignoring the waves far below, no stopping for anything, let alone a laggard, then it can become too much.

Fortunately Lord Howe holds many more miles of trails – all well sign-posted – which weave between the palms and the pandanus, the spreading banyan and the

Above The Lord Howe Island woodhen, Tricholimnus sylvestrus *was brought back from the brink of extinction.*

Below *Visitors can rent a bicycle and ride along Lagoon Road, the island's main road; this is a good way to get around.*

Opposite *Looking back from Mt Gower, the view over Mt Lidgbird, the blue lagoon and the reef is breathtaking.*

tropical hardwoods, to reach isolated beaches or less perilous vantage points high up under the lava cliffs where petrels, terns and tropical birds swoop and soar.

The Muttonbird Point, Goat House Cave, Boat Harbour tracks diverge on top of Smoking Tree Ridge. The names are more evocative than the reality, although aerial pandanus roots and brick-red fungus growing out of apple-green moss enliven these shadowy glades. Staghorn and bird's nest ferns flourish without the assiduous care and watering they demand in suburban homes on the mainland.

On the flank of Mt Lidgbird, the nearer peak, the Goat House Cave is reached by another ropeway clinging to an exposed cliff face. Birdsong fills the air, from the melodious calls of cavorting seabirds to the crack of something very like the eastern whipbird, associated with temperate forests on the mainland. You can see right across Lord Howe Island, all its bays and

forests, to the northernmost tip. Back on the sheltered lagoon side of the island, a quick dip presents a seductive option. Weave up onto the grass, point the bike at one of the ubiquitous bike racks, rip off the gear and in you go. You'll be dry before reaching home.

Twenty kilometres (13 miles) offshore Ball's Pyramid soars 500m (1800ft) out of the ocean like a drowned cathedral, impregnable and unattainable.

Weather permitting, Keith Galloway skippers his 13m (42ft) game-fishing launch *B-Centauri* out to the freshwater springs at Sylph's Hole or Erscott's Hole or even as far away as Elizabeth Reef.

From the air, the reefs resemble human embryos, curled in an almost foetal position. These jaws of death have trapped 40 ships over the last two centuries.

Galloway produces an album full of shots of happy parties posing with huge, silvery trophies: yellowfin tuna, warehou, the red tomato and lunar cod, the maori cod and the giant lobster, many of them straying south from tropical waters. More trophies await from fishing off the brutally sharp volcanic rock shelves at Old Gulch.

A gentler way to appreciate Lord Howe's underwater marvels is to spend a few hours out aboard the glass-bottomed *Coral Princess*. Tinted a ghostly aqua-marine, the corals of the world's most southerly fringing reef pass underneath while Silver Drummers and Moorish Angels glide silently in between. Manta rays hover close to the bottom. Anemone fish, darting in and out of the anemones, which repel most other species, exemplify the symbiotic relationships, the mutual interdependence of marine life.

Fiji

GRAHAM SIMMONS

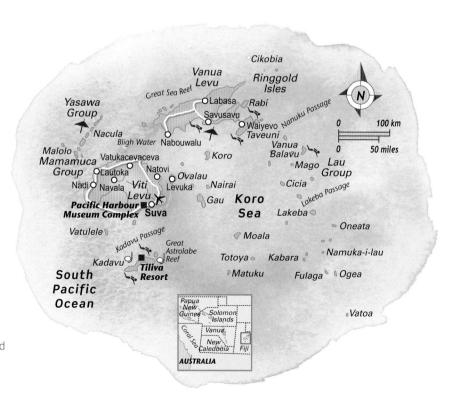

*I*n the rugged Nakauvadra Ranges of Fiji's main island, Viti Levu, Chief Semesa of Vatukacevaceva issues a warning to would-be four-wheel drivers: 'If you don't get my blessing to go into the hills, the ancestral spirits will chase you down again!' To back up his words, the chief produces a sacred stone, a perfect sphere the size and weight of a cannon-ball, which seems to ring in echo to his warning. The scenic Nakauvadra Range is home to the ancestral gods, in particular the serpent god Degei, still revered and worshipped by the locals despite the introduction of Christianity. According to legend, Degei and Lutonasobusobu were leaders of the first people to arrive in Fiji. Their tribe was said to have come from Thebes in Egypt, from where they travelled up the Nile to Tanganyika (now Tanzania), and then eventually migrated from Africa to Fiji. Travelling inland from the coast, they settled at the foot of the Nakauvadra Range, and founded the village of Vatukacevaceva.

A cultural interpreter tells a similar story at the Pacific Harbour museum complex, southeast of Suva. But the narrator adds further details to the story: many died during the trip across the Indian Ocean, and to replace them, the travellers raided Indonesia and Papua New Guinea where few were able to resist. The only people smart enough to escape the invading hordes were the Australian aborigines, who knew in advance of the convoy's approach and watched silently from hiding places in the hills.

Whatever the truth of this story, the Fijians have always been close to their gods. Patricia Page, who grew up in Fiji, says: 'A priest or bete was not only a prophet and a witchdoctor with healing powers, he was considered a god. He and the gods had the same mana or power'.

These legends and beliefs may leave first-time visitors to Fiji scratching their heads; but undoubtedly, the mystique of this 'world-within-a-country' leaves an indelible imprint. Travelling in all directions throughout the wide-flung islands of the Fijian archipelago, the visitor meets with the last Polynesian settlements in an over-whelmingly Melanesian country. You will encounter communities where, despite recent coups and their resulting chaos, Indian immigrants and the native Melanesian and Polynesian peoples coexist in harmony; and marvel at the relaxed, laid-back awareness of the Fijian people.

Fiji's islands are scattered over a vast area of the Pacific Ocean, some 1,290,000km^2 (50,400sq.miles) in extent. To explore the archipelago, it's convenient to follow the lead of one of Fiji's two major domestic airlines – Sunflower Air, and explore the islands in clockwise fashion, as they radiate out like petals from the centre of a big 'sunflower'.

The main island of Viti Levu, at the centre of the 'flower', is some 10,400km^2 (4060sq.miles) in area. The country's first and third biggest cities respectively – Suva and Nadi – are located at opposite ends of Viti Levu, like sentinels guarding against enemy invasion. Flying into Nadi or Suva, the visitor catches a first glimpse of the near-surreal landscape, with the swirling clouds and the hilltops seeming to be locked in an intimate embrace; it is difficult to tell where the earth ends and the sky begins.

Viti Levu has some excellent resorts, particularly on the southern coast between Nadi and Suva. But possibly the most interesting region of Viti Levu is the interior, where people still live in the traditional manner. Navala village, along the Ba River, is one of the oldest traditional villages, its thatch-roofed houses the most authentic of all the surviving interior settlements. Nearer to Nadi, the new

Right *A Fijian man, who works at the Pacific Harbour resort, is dressed in a grass skirt and wears a head dress made of leaves.*

Opposite *Fiji at sunset epitomises the ultimate island experience; the hustle and bustle of the world is far, far away.*

Koroyanitu National Heritage Park in the hinterland of Fiji's second biggest city Lautoka, has it all — forests and waterfalls, hiking trails, and mountain streams great for swimming — plus the opportunity to stay with villagers and experience life in a Fijian highland community.

In the east, the Fijian capital Suva is a funky south seas port. 'Love it and loathe it' is the reaction of many visitors, who can easily be overwhelmed by its mix of natural beauty and urban squalor; full-on religious fervour side-by-side with rampant crime; and both the best and worst of what the outside world has brought to this enigmatic nation.

Just 20km (12.4 miles) along one of the 'petals', east of the Viti Levu port of Natovi, the 100km^2 (40sq.miles) of the historic island of Ovalau is home to what was Fiji's first capital, Levuka. Today, Levuka and its environs are quiet and lazily peaceful, with great views from Gun Rock over a splendid harbour. Some interesting developments are happening at village level; for the isolated village of Naikorokoro is setting up a no-fishing reserve — a coral reef protection zone — on a 43km^2 (17sq.mile) portion of their traditional fishing area, with the eventual aim of establishing a Marine Park.

Further east from Ovalau, at the eastern extremity of the Fiji Islands, is the Lau Group — 57 islands covering a vast area of ocean — nearly one-third of the entire country. Vanua Balavu is the biggest island in the Lau group, home to the last remnant in Fiji of a once great Tongan empire, and the birthplace of Fijian Prime Minister Laisenia Qarase.

Tevita (David) Fotofili, from the Tongan bloodline, who conquered the eastern Fijian islands in the early 1800s, is a dynamic character who seems a little constrained by the borders of his island home. 'Fifteen years ago', he says, 'I went to Australia in search of my great-great grandfather, the first Tongan-Fijian missionary to travel abroad,' he says. 'I discovered that he had been mortally speared by Aborigines.'

Sawana, the southern 'precinct' of Lomaloma village, is today the last Tongan village in the whole of Fiji. Distinguishing signs are the rounded edges of houses, typical of Tongan architecture, and the woven palm-leaf 'aprons' worn on Sundays and on ceremonial occasions. Church on Sunday morning is a mixture of some very powerful singing and fire-and-brimstone preaching — mercifully, the visitor is likely to be blissfully ignorant of what the preacher is saying.

Above left *A local man walks along the shore with freshly hand-picked coconuts from the trees on Kadavu Island, Fiji.*
Above right *The abundant corals, sponges and marine species in the seas around the islands make the area a diver's paradise.*
Opposite *The clear turquoise water makes it possible for you to see the coral under water without leaving your canoe.*

To the south of Vanua Balavu, are the 'teardrop' little islands of Namalata and Susui. In a cave just above the high-tide at Ravi-Ravi Beach lives Kumidamu, the God of the Shells. 'When the Japanese first came here, they wanted to buy the island', says Fotofili, with just a hint of hyperbole, 'because just about every kind of shell in the world can be found here'.

In the south of Fiji, Kadavu Island dominates the seascape. From the air, Kadavu looks like a long, spindly bull-ant set down in the sea, with a mountainous spine

ending at the western end in a big dome. The waters lapping over the shore-coral on the northern side of the island are a brilliant turquoise and aquamarine all in one, so vivid that even a paint company's advertising agent couldn't find words to describe the hue.

The diving and snorkelling on Kadavu Island (particularly at the eastern tip) are, along with Vanua Balavu, among the very best sites in the world. Within three minutes' swim from the beach are soft and hard corals that stun in their multiform beauty. And the Great Astrolabe Reef, just five minutes by boat from the low-key resort Albert's Place, is world renowned.

Other dive resorts also grace the shores of Kadavu Island. More up-market, also at the eastern tip of the island, Tiliva Resort is a newcomer to the scene. Diving, snorkelling, kayaking and medicinal plant tours are just a few of the activities available.

In the west of Fiji, and just offshore from Viti Levu, the Mamanuca Group is probably the most accessible of all the smaller Fijian islands. Dick Smith was the pioneer of resort islands in Fiji, and now owns Musket Cove Resort on Mamanuca's Malololailai (or 'Little Malolo') Island. First coming to Fiji in 1959, he was captivated by the place. 'It's the best cruising yacht zone in the Pacific', he says. 'The Cook Islands and Samoa are too spread out, as are the Solomons and Vanuatu. But here in Fiji, you can cruise comfortably in complete safety among sheltered lagoons.'

There's a shop on Malololailai, the Traders' Store, that is reminiscent of a 19th-century south seas trading post. At low tide, villagers from the more traditional 'Big' Malolo Island walk or wade across the strait between the two islands, dodging corals, sea-snakes and starfish, to do their shopping. From the top of the biggest hill on Malolo, the views over Malololailai are spectacular indeed.

The Yasawa Island chain, at '10 o'clock' on the sunflower dial, looks like a chain of little droplets flung off the main island Viti Levu. One of the prettiest of the islands is Nacula, its beaches more than usually picture-postcard, with hidden treasures like the Sawa-i-Lau Cave, high in the hills. On Nacula, Oarsman's Bay Lodge comes with a high recommendation.

Over four degrees latitude north of Nacula, and with the nearest land 500km (300 miles) away, the remote Rotuma Island is a fusion of (mainly) Polynesian and Melanesian cultures. On Rotuma, Methodism is strong — and so is the kava, made from green plants that somehow deliver a more potent hit. It is said that the islanders lost the ability to make sea-going canoes because they had no desire to go anywhere, and the few visitors that make it here invariably say that they can understand why.

Vanua Levu is the second biggest island in Fiji, with an area of 5555km^2 (2170sq.miles). Its capital, Savusavu, is very much alive, and dressed to kill — dressed in saris, sulus, swimsuits, and everything in between — a dynamic population mix of Fijians, Indians and Chinese, and Savusavu attracts a large 'floating' population of sailing enthusiasts, divers and beach-lovers, with a superb new marina and cruise centre fronting the safe haven of Savusavu Bay.

Savusavu Bay is great for kayaking. Picture, if you will, a bay that takes the form of a fractal image, where each arm bifurcates, trifurcates and multifurcates into dozens of mini-bays, each seemingly a replica of the main bay. Little wonder, then, that an exploratory trip becomes totally engrossing.

The last petal on the big Fiji sunflower belongs to many visitors' very favourite island. Taveuni, the 'Garden Island', is a riot of lush flower-studded

Above *Enjoy a stroll along the Lavena coast of Taveuni, but take extra care as the rocks are slippery.*

Opposite *The old Copra Shed Wharf on Savusava Island has now become a fashionable marina and tourist attraction.*

greenery, and is traversed by the 180-degree meridian.

Cyclone Amy, which swept through the island in early 2003, is proof that nature respects neither datelines nor meridians. Fortunately, the excellent dive resorts of the island are now back to normal. Taveuni's Garden Island Resort and its associated Aqua-Trek dive operation, just north of Waiyevo village, were respectively awarded the title of 'best dive operator' and 'best dive resort in the world' in 2003 by the prestigious US magazine *Scuba Diving International*. The red-and-white tagimoucia flower that is the hallmark of Taveuni Island gives its name

to the sacred Lake Tagimoucia, an ethereal crater lake 823m (2700ft) high, accessible only by a strenuous hike through dense forests from Des Voeux Peak (but it is just possible to ascend Des Voeux Peak by four-wheel drive, only in the hands of an expert local driver).

On the east coast of Taveuni Island, the Lavena Coastal Walk is a must. This is part of the recently re-branded Bouma National Heritage Park. Also on the east coast of Taveuni, the new Waitabu Marine Reserve offers excellent snorkelling, with soft corals that must rate among the finest of their kind on the planet.

Back on shore at Waitabu, the visitor is likely treated to a veritable feast. As the kava bowl is passed around, the guitarists get deeper and deeper into their music — until finally, the band breaks into *Isa Lei*, surely the most poignant farewell song ever put to music. At this point, just as at the impending time of departure from Fiji, there is unlikely to be a dry eye in the house.

Bora Bora

ROBIN MCKELVIE

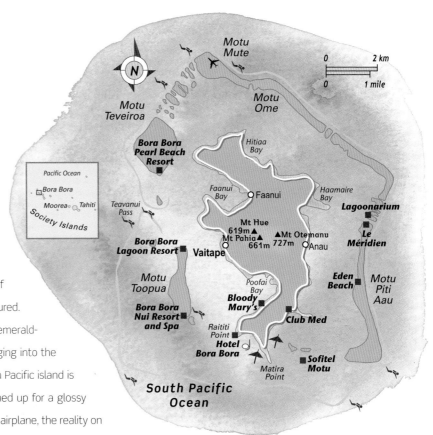

egend has it that the captains of the first ships to sight Bora Bora found themselves stranded alone as their crews flung themselves overboard into the island's welcoming arms, never to return. This Pacific Ocean outpost also fired the fertile imaginations of painter Paul Gauguin and writer Robert Louis Stevenson, as well as fellow literary giant James A Michener, who once hailed Bora Bora 'the most beautiful island in the world'. After even the briefest of dalliances with this Polynesian hideaway, it is hard not to become similarly enraptured.

The self-styled 'Paradise of the Pacific' is the Treasure Island cliché: an emerald-green baize of rainforest streams down from the island's volcanic peaks, merging into the turquoise water that surrounds the isle and its smaller islets. The entire South Pacific island is laced with cotton-wool soft sand in a scene that looks like it has been touched up for a glossy tourist brochure or for a computer screensaver. If it all looks too good from the airplane, the reality on the ground is even more impressive. Somehow in Bora Bora the sand is whiter, the sea a deeper shade of blue, the rainforest impossibly lush and the peaks vault above even more ruggedly than they did from the air.

The first thing that visitors see when they approach Bora Bora is the hulking peak of Mt Otemanu, which soars 727m (2380ft) above sea level in a grand greeting gesture. It is dramatically backed up by Mt Hue which rises to 619m (2000ft) and Mt Pahia which reaches a height of 661m (2165ft), two further peaks that reach for the sky from the blanket of thick green rainforest that covers most of the island. This mountainous core is surrounded by the trademark lagoon, which is itself enclosed by a string of small islets (*motus*), some of them little more than brief slivers of sand. Although it is only 29km (18 miles) in circumference, Bora Bora is Tahiti's real star.

Opposite The over-water bungalows making up the Bora Bora hotel, have all the facilities of a luxury hotel while fitting in perfectly with the natural environment.
Below To get the full Bora Bora experience, take a cruise across the lagoon on one of the yachts – it's a great way to enjoy the majestic scenery.

The island is set adrift in the Pacific Ocean 241km (150 miles) from Tahiti, the eponymous main island in the chain, and its tiny population of just over 5000 enjoys a real sense of isolation. Getting here either requires a long boat trip or a beach hopping flight from Pape'ete, Tahiti's capital. Although the islands are in effect a French colony (the Tahitian, or 'Society', islands are part of the larger political entity of French Polynesia), the influence of Paris, or anywhere else for that matter, seems a long way away out here. Bora Bora after all is over 5632km (3500 miles) from Sydney, 6100km (3800 miles) from Los Angeles and 8690km (5400 miles) from Tokyo.

While the period of French rule is well documented, the hazy origins of the island's original inhabitants are less clear. No one can put an exact date to when the Polynesian people embarked, most probably from South East Asia, on their epic sea voyage and washed ashore on Bora Bora. They soon held sway over the island, with a rustic civilization based on basic cultivation and fishing from outrigger canoes. Tales of cannibalism swirl around this shadowy past and this ritual practice certainly occurred elsewhere in the archipelago, so it may well have darkened Bora Bora too.

Most of the first European visitors to Tahiti, though, have a more than favourable impression of the island and its people. Captain Cook reported a race of

Above The lagoon's vibrant marine life includes schools of beautifully coloured double-saddle butterfly fish.

Right For the inexperienced scuba diver, snorkelling across the shallow waters of the lagoon is just as rewarding.

'noble savages' and eulogized the beautiful bare-breasted women, who were apparently only too generous in their favours to passing sailors. This friendliness was often taken advantage of as the cultures clashed and the European new arrivals did not fully understand the indigenes, let alone the name of the island, calling it mistakenly Bora Bora, when the actual moniker is Pora Pora, which translates as 'first born'.

Christian missionaries came to Bora Bora in the 18th century, spreading religion and soon putting an end to the worst of the debauchery and the pagan rituals. As the number of European missionaries increased and traders joined them, France took over the entire French Polynesian archipelago in 1842, propping up Queen Pomare IV as a figurehead ruler for the next 50 years. In the 20th century, nuclear testing became a major issue between the Polynesians and the French, but the

series of tests never troubled Bora Bora, and the tensions have eased of late throughout French Polynesia as a whole.

Bora Bora is still a land where reality and imagination merge, where the lines become blurred; the land where French painter Paul Gauguin painted some of his finest masterpieces and Scottish writer Robert Louis Stevenson, author of *Treasure Island*, came to feed his outlandish imaginative wanderings. On Bora Bora, the fictional Treasure Island seems every bit as real as the *Mutiny on the Bounty* – the

notorious mutiny that actually descended on the Tahitian archipelago in 1789, when Fletcher Christian rose against Captain Bligh and his supporters, exiling them to their fate in a small boat. Perhaps the most famous literary evocation of Bora Bora came from American writer James A Michener, who waxed lyrical about 'the most beautiful island in the world'.

One of the reasons that Bora Bora retains much of its original allure is that it remains genuinely unspoiled, a reality not just a tourist office slogan. There are more bedrooms in some Las Vegas hotels than there are on all of the 118 islands of Tahiti, and Hawaii gets more tourists in two weeks than the whole archipelago gets in a year. Some quaint traditions remain today, such as the 'mail boxes' which are actually designed not for letters, but for the sticks of French bread that are a local staple – you have to go to the post office to get your mail! Then there are the Tiare, which are fragrant, white flowers that help keep Bora Borans' love lives in check. Wearing it in your left ear means that you are spoken for and in the right, well, let's just say it means you are open to the kind of amorous liaisons that Bora Bora has always been synonymous with.

The best way to get a real feel for the island is by taking a jeep or a bicycle for a ride around the island. A complete circuit of the island is only 32km (20 miles) and can easily be negotiated in a day, though plenty of time should be left to allow a stop-off at deserted strips of sand or to savour a cool drink in one of the island's rustic watering holes. The road is easy to follow, with a few smaller trails branching off it that just beg to be explored, though drivers should beware of being too adventurous as a solid surface can soon give way to muddied quagmire after heavy rain.

Taking to the Pacific Ocean waters is another excellent way of exploring Bora Bora, especially when the famed ocean breezes are in short supply. It can be a little crowded in the water but not with other people, as this aquatic escape boasts myriad sweeping sting rays, hurtling sea turtles, massive moray eels and even steely eyed reef sharks. Experienced divers can scuba dive in the lagoon, but often snorkelling is just as rewarding, as the shallow waters mean that you only need dip your head beneath the surface to get straight into the action. Visitors wanting to keep their feet dry can hop on a boat. Trips range from laidback sunset cruises with a sundowner cocktail through to adrenaline-pumping sport fishing adventures in search of the big fish that lie just outside the lagoon.

Then there is surfing and water skiing or wind surfing and kayaking, with activities for everyone in the family. This surprises some first-time visitors as, although Bora Bora is mainly renowned as the ultimate honeymoon escape, it also embraces families looking to really get away from it all. The privations of beach huts and overbearing tropical heat have been greatly tempered since Gauguin

Opposite Bora Borans are justly famous for the friendliness and hospitality that they display towards the many visitors to their beautiful island.

Below Bora Bora's world famous beaches make it the perfect destination for those who wish to laze in the sun and take in the picturesque scenery.

and Stevenson sweated ashore from the lagoon. Today's visitors enjoy a much more comfortable experience as Bora Bora is awash with some of the smartest, most luxurious hotels in the world. The local authorities have made sure that they have been designed to fit in with the natural environment, with many incorporating traditional Polynesian architecture. Cindy Crawford, Harrison Ford and Pamela Anderson are among those said to have indulged in a break in the over-water thatched bungalows, which come complete with four-poster beds, glass coffee tables that reveal the marine life below and your own private steps down to the lagoon waters.

While some of the most lavish hotels have their own boutiques, real retail addicts may prefer to venture out in search of more esoteric souvenirs. A Bora Boran specialty is the remarkable black pearl. These jet black treasures are found within the Tahitian Mother of Pearl, but as they are found in only 1 in 15,000 pearl oysters in the wild, they are now cultivated in Tahiti. Also dotted around the island are small galleries where the work of local painters and artisans is on sale, with plenty of opportunity to pick up something genuinely unique that is guaranteed to get the neighbours talking back home.

Few of the guests who stay in Bora Bora's world-class hotels today are aware of the island's darkest secret. Deep in the densest recesses of the rainforest lurks a legacy of the island's all too recent history. During the 1940s, 5000 foreigners who disrupted the pastoral calm with their bulldozers and machine guns invaded the island. The invaders did not come to terrorize the local population — they were American servicemen sent to bolster the island's defences in the bloody fight against the Japanese.

You can still find people living on Bora Bora who have photograph albums tucked away in their cupboards, full of black-and-white shots of GIs toiling away bare-chested in the Pacific heat. Today few visitors will encounter any visible scars from those days, but if you delve up the mountain trails you can uncover rusting big howitzers looming over the lagoon. One positive legacy has been the large runway left by the American forces on one of the *motus* in the lagoon, which now provides the island's main link with the outside world and a way in for tourists who are not keen on the long boat trip from Tahiti.

When the American servicemen were in town, Bora Bora's nightlife was unsurprisingly quite a raucous affair, but these days things are far more sedate. Given the quality of the hotels, many visitors choose just to take in sunset in their over-water bungalows or eat in a hotel restaurant that marries Tahitian food with French colonial styles. Outside of the hotels the beaches are the obvious place for a private picnic, while those in search of more social evenings can choose from a sprinkling of informal bars. The most renowned is Bloody Marys, which since 1979 has been keeping up the best Bora Boran traditions of hospitality, by serving up freshly grilled seafood and expertly mixed cocktails for island guests and waylaid sailors alike.

The quintessential Bora Bora experience is, of course, taking a cruise around the *motus*, preferably in one of the older yachts that drift around the lagoon. As you sink deep into your hammock and the sails billow into life with a soothing South Pacific breeze, you will find your mind swirling away. Gazing over the side of the boat as the sun illuminates the volcanic peaks of Bora Bora, it is easy to imagine the ghosts of Gauguin and Stevenson dancing across the skyline, and it is more than tempting to follow in the footsteps of the first sailors who slipped overboard and lost themselves on Bora Bora forever.

Above Sun-drenched beaches, friendly people, crystal-clear waters and the vibrant sounds of calypso music are hallmarks of the islands of the Caribbean.

The Caribbean and North America

Grenada

GARY BUCHANAN

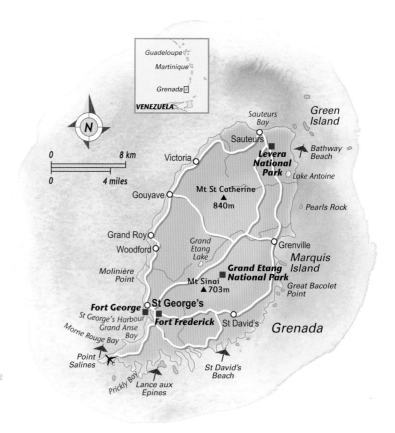

Grenada is supremely seductive; from the powdery beaches and restful hotels of the southwest to the bustling fishing port of Gouyave in St John's parish in the northwest, from the inaccessible southeast with its patchwork of little farms, to the photogenic capital of St George's. The rich aroma of cinnamon, nutmeg, cloves and other spices hovers over the fertile, volcanic hills; little wonder this teardrop-shaped Caribbean gem is known as its 'Spice Island'.

The three-island state that comprises Grenada, Carriacou and Petite Martinique is located in the Eastern Caribbean at the southern extremity of the Windward Islands, 160km (100 miles) north of Venezuela. To the north lie St Vincent and the Grenadines; to the south is Trinidad and Tobago. Grenada is the largest of the three islands, and is 18km (12 miles) wide and 34km (21 miles) long. The total area is 344km² (133sq.miles). The highest point is Mt St Catherine at 840m (2757ft).

When Christopher Columbus discovered the island in 1498 it was inhabited by Amerindians who called their island Camerhogue, but Columbus renamed the island Conception. However, passing Spanish sailors found its lush green hills so evocative of Andalusia that they rejected this name in favour of Granada. The French then called it La Grenade, with the British finally changing it to Grenada.

In 1650 a French expedition from Martinique landed. Hostilities broke out with the Caribs fighting a succession of losing battles until the last surviving Indians jumped to their death off a precipice in the north of the island. The French named the spot Le Morne de Sauteurs (Leaper's Hill).

The French struggled unsuccessfully to keep the island from falling to the British for the next 90 years. Fort George and Fort Frederick, which have a commanding position overlooking St George's harbour, are relics of these hostilities. Finally under the Treaty of Versailles in 1783, the island was permanently ceded to the British, who immediately imported large numbers of slaves from Africa and established sugar plantations.

In 1877 Grenada became a Crown Colony, and in 1967 joined the British Commonwealth before gaining independence in 1974. The tri-island state remains within the British Commonwealth as an independent nation, with the Governor General representing Her Majesty, The Queen.

Average temperatures range from 24°C (75°F) to 30°C (87°F), tempered by cooling trade winds. The lowest temperatures occur between November and February. Because of Grenada's remarkable topography, the island also experiences climatic changes according to altitude. The driest season is between January and May; the rainy season from June to December.

Grenada's largest festival is Carnival, held on the second weekend in August; it includes calypso and steel band competitions, a pageant and a 'jump-up'. The Spice Island Billfish Tournament held in January is an important date for anglers; while the Carriacou Regatta in July is a magnet for sailors throughout the Caribbean.

The picturesque hillside town of St George's surrounds the deep horseshoe-shaped harbour and is renowned as one of the prettiest in the Caribbean. It is the very quintessence of colonial Caribbean: pastel-hued 19th-century Creole houses intertwined with 18th century French provincial houses; a tumult of bougainvillea lining the waterfront of the Carenage inner harbour, where ship's

chandlers and ramshackle warehouses service schooners swaying in the hypnotic air; three solid brown churches nestling among English Georgian houses, square edifices of red brickwork faded by the tropical sun.

The winding maze of streets and alleyways that climb upwards from the Carenage pass under wrought-iron balconies supported by hefty beams of wood; balconies draped in bougainvillea and bright with trailing geraniums. The sensation of illicit, secretive, hidden activities is tempered by policemen directing traffic at chaotic intersections. The Catholic Cathedral, Parliament Building, St Joseph's Convent and the Presentation Brothers' College are popular attractions, but most tourists head to the colourful Spice Market and the Grenada National Museum. Here hotchpotch exhibits include fragments of Amerindian pottery, an old rum still, and a grubby marble bathtub that once belonged to Empress Josephine.

The hilltop Fort George, originally built by the French in 1705 when it was known as Fort Royal, has fine views from the harbour's western promontory across the town's red and pink-tiled rooftops and church spires. The extensive defences

Right Visitors can spend time at the busy market on a Saturday and choose from a variety of fresh fruit and vegetables.

Opposite A view of the waterfront of Carenage's inner harbour, enclosed by St George's English Georgian houses and brown churches; the buildings' roofs are all faded by the sun.

include cannons still in use to fire salutes. In the fort's inner courtyard there are bullet holes in the basketball pole made by the firing squad that executed Maurice Bishop – leader of the People's Revolutionary Government, who led an armed, almost bloodless, revolution in 1979, seizing power from the government. The spot is marked by fading graffiti reading 'No Pain, No Gain, Brother'.

Perched on a ridge 244m (800ft) above sea level, the late 18th-century Fort Frederick protects the harbour's eastern entrance and has panoramic views of Grenada's southwestern coastline. The fort is well preserved thanks, in part, to the tragic targeting blunder made during the US invasion of 1983. The Americans intended to hit the fort but mistakenly bombed Fort Matthew, a few hundred yards away, which was being used as a mental hospital at the time of the attack.

There are around 45 superlative beaches edging the sapphirine sea, but the most popular is unquestionably Grand Anse – 1.25km (2 miles) of iridescently white sand lining a sheltered bay on the western (leeward) side of the island. Several hotels have taken advantage of this prime location where there is a variety of water sports and restaurants by the water's edge.

From Grand Anse there are six more 'bounty bar' beaches lining the coastline to the southwestern tip of the island at Point Salines; these are more private than Grand Anse, yet are easily accessible and popular with locals and tourists alike. Families head for Morne Rouge Bay, just south of Grand Anse, where the water is calmer and motorized water-borne activities are prohibited.

The island's east coast is a haven for lovers of secluded beaches. These tend to be off-the-beaten-track and only accessible by four-wheel-drive vehicles. Lance Aux Epines, St David's and Bathway are the most popular beaches on the Atlantic coastline, which can be choppy during some months of the year.

What sets Grenada apart from many other Caribbean islands is the chance to explore the dense hinterland. The pre-eminent area for

Above left *A view of the Grenadine Islands, north of Grenada. The Grenadines is a group of about 600 small islands, each more than making up for its diminutive size with a rich and diverse scenery.*
Left *For those who prefer to spend time away from the madding crowds, there are lush green forests and calming waterfalls to enjoy.*
Opposite *Grand Anse Beach is a typical island beach – blue waters, palm trees and colourful yachts 'parked' by the shoreline.*

hiking and trekking is in the rainforest around the extinct volcano that is Grand Etang Lake in the centre of the island. Most of the Windward Islands in the Caribbean share the same volcanic origin and, while most are extinct, many of them have active geothermal activity within their territories. Grenada is no exception, but over the centuries, its volcanoes have been reduced to eroded remnants, claimed by the rainforest.

From the Grand Etang National Park Visitors' Centre there are self-guided hikes through tableaux of divergent flora and fauna. Each marked trail encircles the azure waters of the crater-lake at 586m (1900ft). The Seven Sisters Trail is a more ambitious, but incredibly rewarding, rainforest trek past secreted waterfalls and pools.

The 182ha (450-acre) Levera National Park is without a doubt Grenada's most scenic and spectacular coastal area. Its peaceful, picture-postcard lagoon is one of the most important wildlife habitats on the island, where the mangrove swamp is a haven for birds. There is an outstanding coral reef, but witnessing sea turtles hatching on the beaches is to experience nature at its most sublime.

Grenada certainly spans the full spectrum of Caribbean life. It is a destination that offers much more than a lotus-eater's paradigm of paradise. Hotels are full of local character, as opposed to temples of indulgence; food employs flavoursome local produce, rather than anodyne international cuisine. This is a destination where spending time in the towns and national parks is an unalloyed delight, and no opportunity should be missed to meet the ebullient Grenadians for an idiomatic take on local culture and history.

Martinique

GARY BUCHANAN

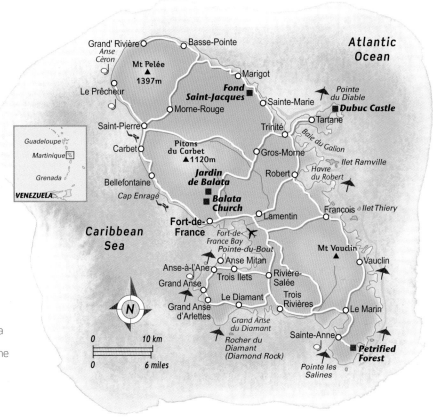

artinique is large by Caribbean standards. It is also an island of contrasts; the north is more dramatic and interesting than the cultivated and industrialised south. The active Mount Pelée volcano dominates the landscape and spreads a cloak of mysticism across it; in its foothills, the rainforest glows and waterfalls hang like sparkling frayed rope. Island-wide, the all-pervading chic of La Belle France and sensuous Caribbean lifestyle make for a heady combination.

The French Overseas Département of Martinique is the northernmost of the Windward Island group of the Lesser Antilles. Measuring fifty miles [80 kilometres] long and 39km (24 miles) wide, this emerald green isle, surrounded by a fringe of gold, is situated between the islands of St Lucia, 29km (18 miles) to the south, and Dominica 37km (23 miles) to the north.

The total area of the island is 1080km² (417sq.miles) and is characterized by a scalloped coastline and a mountainous terrain which rises steeply from the sea. The dormant Mount Pelée is the country's highest point at 1397m (4583ft); on 8 May 1902 this volcano erupted and completely destroyed the city of Saint-Pierre, killing 30,000 inhabitants.

Christopher Columbus first landed in Martinique in 1502 and called it 'the most beautiful country in the world'. He found the island inhabited by Carib Indians who once shared the land with Arawaks before being driven out. The Caribs named the island Madinina, 'Island of Flowers'. Three decades later a party of French settlers, led by Pierre Belain d'Esnambuc, landed and established a small fort and settlement in 1635, naming it Saint-Pierre, the island's first capital; which soon became known as 'Little Paris of the West Indies'.

Colonization proceeded swiftly and by 1640 the French had extended their stronghold as far south as Fort-de-France. The British invaded and took the island from 1794 until 1815. During this period of prosperity the sugar planters sold their crops to the British markets rather than the French.

The French administration was later re-established but coincided with a decline in the sugar cane market; consequently the plantation owners lost much of their political power and by 1848 slavery was brought to an end. In 1946 the island, together with Guadeloupe, Saint-Barthélémy and the French half of Saint-Martin, became an Overseas Department of France (department d'outre-mer), and their citizens French nationals.

Martinique enjoys a tropical climate; there is a wet season between June and October and the southern area of the island tends to be drier. November to May are

Below Fort-de-France at night is ablaze with light; by day you can explore its many well-preserved monuments and museums.

Opposite Balata Church (Basilica of the Sacred Heart) towers above the island's trees and is overlooked by Mt Pelée.

cooler, drier months when the *alizés* breezes blow from the northeast. Average temperatures range from 21°C (70°F) to 29°C (84°F) between January and March, and 23°C (73°F) to 31°C (88°F) between June and October. The Caribbean side is drier than the Atlantic coast.

Martinique has a five-day Mardi Gras Carnival prior to Ash Wednesday. The streets fill with rum-fuelled revellers and there are costume parades, music and dancing. Saint-Pierre commemorates the 8th May eruption of Mount Pelée with live jazz and a candlelit procession from the cathedral. The Tour de la Martinique is a week-long cycle race held in mid-July; the Tour des Yoles Rondes is a week-long traditional sail-boat race held in August, and there's a biannual Jazz Festival and Guitar Festival.

Creole traditions coexist in harmony with the ubiquitous Gallic influence; indeed

Below *Extravagant costumes reveal the islanders' 'joie de vivre' and the enthusiasm with which they celebrate festivals. Move over, Rio! Carnival fever on Martinique is no less impressive and the festivities just as enthusiastic.*

Left *A view of Mt Pelée Volcano in the distance is framed by the lush, tropical foliage of the island of Martinique.*

Opposite *Enjoy a stroll in the Le Jardin de Balata botanical garden, which has a rich variety of exotic flowers and tropical trees.*

it is often said that Martinique is a slice of France set down in the tropics. Islanders wear Paris fashions, eat croissants, and read France-Antilles. The Afro-French beguine, originated in Martinique in the 1930s, but it is the more contemporary French West Indian music, zouk, that is omnipresent in bars and cafés.

The capital Fort-de-France is a modern city best explored on foot. Patisseries, couturiers and jewellers rub shoulders with pavement cafés selling Ricard and Bière Lorraine in narrow, iron-balconied streets. While the ambiance is engaging and in parts entrancing, in truth it has more in common with Graham Greene than Jean-Paul Sartre.

Sails flapping in the harbour create an ever-changing backdrop at the main square of Savane, a waterfront park with 18th-century townhouses, fountains, and statue of Empress Josephine. At the lively market, by the waterfront Park Floral, there is a kaleidoscope of colourful island produce. The main tourist centre, Pointe-du-Bout, is a peninsula jutting out into Fort-de-France Bay, with a golf course, casino, bevy of hotels, and scores of restaurants.

One of Martinique's most renowned tourist attractions is the Musée de la Pagerie in the village of Trois Ilets. It's filled with mementos recounting the lavish lifestyle of the Empress Josephine who was born here in 1763. There's a fascinating collection of furniture, including the bed that Napoleon's wife slept in until her departure for France at the age of 16. There are portraits of the couple, invitations to Paris soirées, medals, and passionate missives from the lovelorn Napoleon.

Fort-de-France divides the island into two distinct regions: beaches to the south, history to the north. The offshore landmark, Diamond Rock, is sometimes dubbed the Caribbean Gibraltar. It rises 185m (600ft) from the sea, and was used as a fort by the British at the beginning of the 19th century.

The stereotyped Caribbean beaches of mother-of-pearl sand abutting indolent, turquoise water, shaded by swaying palms are here aplenty. Martinique's finest stretch of pristine sand of Les Salines, at the southern tip of the island, enjoys an untrammelled setting; while Anse-à-l'Ane, Anse Mitan, and Grande Anse d'Arlettes on the Caribbean shore, are more remote. On the Atlantic coast, black-sand beaches provide protected coves and good waves for watersports. Game fishing is world-class, while snorkelling is best around Grand Anse and Sainte-Anne.

Great snorkelling is also on offer between Saint-Pierre and Anse Cèron in the north. During the 1902 eruption more than a dozen ships were sunk in Saint-Pierre Bay which offers scuba-divers an unrivalled underwater environment. Other good dive spots are Cap Enragé where underwater caves are the habitat of colourful fish and lobsters.

The former capital of Saint-Pierre is a shadow of its former self. Following the eruption, the Martinicians began rebuilding this New World Pompeii; sadly vestiges of this fin-de-siècle city have been engulfed in tropical foliage and it has fallen into an elegiac desuetude. Indeed a vivid imagination is required to rekindle images of French-colonial villas lining elegant boulevards.

Carbet, just south of Saint-Pierre, is where Columbus landed in 1502; it is also the home of the Musée Gauguin. Reproductions of works such as *Bord de Mer* and *L'Anse Turin – avec les raisiniers*, which he painted on the grey-sand beach of Anse Turin during his five-month stay in 1887, are on display. The Route de la Trace follows a trail blazed by 17th-century Jesuits into the mountains north of Fort-de-France. It winds through a rainforest along the eastern flanks of the volcanic peaks of Pitons du Carbet. A short drive away is Balata Church, a scaled-down replica of the Sacré-Coeur Basilica in Paris, where there are views across Fort-de-France to La Pointe-du-Bout. Further on is Jardin de Balata, a botanical garden laced with paths winding through tropical trees and exotic flowers.

Perhaps nothing so epitomises the history of Martinique as its centuries-old rum-making industry, and nowhere is this better narrated than at the Musée du Rhum, at the Saint-James Plantation distillery. There are displays of steam-powered sugar-making engines, stills, and cane-crushing gears. The tasting room is also an

Above *The fine pristine beach of Les Salines at the southern tip of the island is an ideal setting to kick back, soak up the sun's rays and just socialize.*
Opposite *No prizes for guessing why this offshore landmark is called Diamond Rock! The British used it as a fort at the beginning of the 19th century – its great height and steep cliffs mean it could be defended with relative ease.*

interesting experience! To the north of Sainte-Marie is Fond Saint-Jacques, the site of a Dominican monastery and sugar plantation dating from 1660. It was here that a friar modernised the distilling of rum; the chapel and most of the living quarters are still intact. Martinique delights the senses and refreshes the spirit. This vision of France shimmering under a tropical sun offers a transcendental *je ne sais quoi*. Visitors can share the sea, the landscape, the history; each casts its own spell, each creates its own reverie, together they offer enchantment.

British Virgin Islands

GARY BUCHANAN

Throughout the Caribbean there are groups of islands caressed by gentle winds, ringed by white sand beaches and iridescent waters; but nowhere is there an enchanting cornucopia like the British Virgin Islands. While sharing the indigo sea, the landscape, like the fruit of the cornucopia, offers an Elysian idyll.

Located between the Caribbean Sea and the North Atlantic, the British Virgin Islands encompass 36 islands – of which 20 are uninhabited – and numerous other islets. They have a landmass of 153km² (59sq.miles) and are spread across nearly 2590km² (1000sq.miles) of water. Lying 144km (90 miles) east of Puerto Rico, north of the Leeward Islands, and adjacent to the US Virgin Islands, these

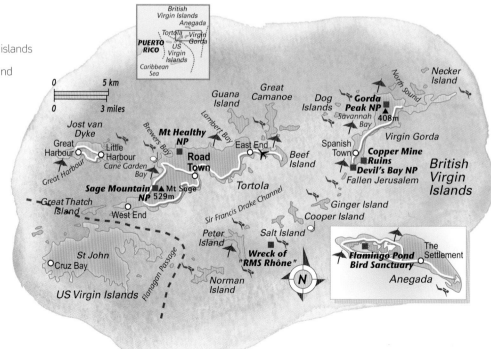

islands are high points on a vast underwater plateau that stretches for more than 112km (70 miles) across the northern Caribbean. All 36 islands are volcanic in origin, save for the coralline Anegada. The largest island, Tortola, at 54km^2 (21sq.miles), is home to this island nation's capital – Road Town. Mt Sage, the highest point in the archipelago, rises to 529m (1716ft).

Columbus encountered this archipelago during his second expedition to the New World in 1493. He named the bountiful islands Islas Virgenes, likening their untouched beauty to the legend of St Ursula and the 11,000 virgins who followed her to martyrdom. But it was gold that the Spanish navigator came in search of, and he soon set his compass for the larger islands of Puerto Rico and Hispaniola.

For another century, these islands remained untouched until the sheltered coves were discovered by pirates and privateers of the 17th and 18th centuries. Some of the era's most notorious brigands are reputed to have launched their raids from these shores, including Blackbeard, Henry Morgan and John Hawkins. Today several of the islands are named for the various picaroons that plundered the Caribbean, such as Jost Van Dyke.

The first European settlers arrived in the 17th century, led by the Spanish who established a copper mine on Virgin Gorda, the remnants of which are still visible. The Dutch constructed a fort at the west end of Tortola, establishing a permanent settlement in 1648. The islands were annexed by the British in 1672, who introduced the two quintessential features of colonialism in the Caribbean: sugar cane and slaves. Between the mid-18th and early 19th centuries the islands prospered, producing sugar, cotton, molasses, spices and rum.

Left *Crystal clear waters, lush green palm trees and golden sands are just a few ways to describe of the stunning Cane Garden Bay; no wonder it's a haven for sailing enthusiasts and sunbathers alike.*

Opposite *Peter Island, private and largely undeveloped, offers many scenic hikes, wonderful beaches and dramatic views of nearby islands in the group.*

Following the emancipation of slaves in the British West Indies in 1834, the plantation holdings were sold to the islands' former slaves, who turned to fishing and farming as a way of life. Over the next century, the territory was administered by a British governor and it was only in 1950 that a Legislative Council was established, leading to the implementation of a new constitution in 1967. The island group remains under British control and is an overseas territory of the UK, with the Governor the representative of Her Majesty, The Queen.

The climate is subtropical, with temperatures ranging from 26°C (79°F) to 31°C (89°F) in the summer and 22°C (72°F) to 28°C (82°F) in winter months. The wettest months are September through November, while the monthly average rainfall is 100mm. Humidity is high, but tempered by the trade winds which are calmer between April and August, resulting in clearer waters for scuba diving. The islands are prone to hurricanes between July and October.

The British Virgin Island's indigenous music is fungi, a form of scratch band music. Heritage and culture are also reflected in art, nowhere more so than the Wall Mural, a long and colourful fresco on Tortola's Fahie Hill. The greatest cultural celebration of the year is the August Emancipation Festival, or Summer Fest, when parades, pageants and local music competitions take place in the Festival Village – a collection of brightly painted wooden booths in the heart of Road Town. The Annual Spring Regatta in April attracts yachters from all over the world; while the HIHO Races in late-June are a magnet for windsurfers.

Tortola, or Turtle Dove, is the hub of the archipelago and home to approximately 17,200 British Virgin Islanders. The capital, Road Town, is located halfway along the island's southern shore and sheltered by an amphitheatre of hills. Well-preserved colonial buildings, their wrought iron balconies draped in jasmine and trailing hibiscus, frame the natural harbour where yachts hardly move in the soporific breeze. Situated on a small bluff to the western end of the harbour is the residence of the islands' British Governor and Old Government House Museum.

West End is a hive of activity with shops, bars, restaurants and marina. The Ferry Dock is the jumping-off-point for trips to Jost Van Dyke, St John and St Thomas. The Marina offers dive trips, day-sails, powerboat rentals, and a provisioning store. It's a popular overnight mooring for charter boats and there's lively nightlife, with the Jolly Roger Restaurant and Pusser's Landing playing Calypso music to the early hours.

Originally built in 1798, the Mt Healthy Windmill is left over from the sugar plantation era, and overlooks the north shore of Tortola. Declared a National Park in 1983, there are spectacular views and picnic tables in the shadow of the ruins of the Boiling House and Overseers' Quarters. In the middle of Road Town, the JR O'Neal Botanic Gardens offer 1.1ha (2.8 acres) of rare and indigenous tropical plants, including 62 species of palms and a cactus garden. Specialized collections of ginger, heliconias and anthuriums are found in the lush rainforest section. From this aerie there are panoramic views of Sir Francis Drake Channel, Virgin Gorda and St John in the USVI.

Established in 1964, the Sage Mountain National Park is a 37ha (92-acre) forest donated to the BVI Government by Lawrence Rockefeller for preservation. Mahoganies, hanging vines and white cedars, as well as rare and endangered plant species, can be seen from a variety of trails and hikes. Shark Bay National Park is located on a dramatic point above Brewer's Bay on the island's north shore.

Ridge Road runs along Tortola's spine and offers panoramic views of the surrounding sea and neighbouring islands. Local homes dot the ridge, many built in traditional West Indian style with verandas, colourful hip roofs and gingerbread trim.

Left *Totola Island's vibrant nightlife and many restaurants offer something for every visitor – and a marvellous end to a busy day relaxing on the beach.*

Opposite *The British Virgin Islands are famous for their sailing waters, which is why there is a host of activities, such as surfing, kayaking and parasailing, for those who prefer to keep their head above water.*

The ruins of 18th and 19th-century buildings associated with the production of rum and sugar can also be seen throughout the island.

The island's north shore contains several beautiful white sand beaches, some accessible by road, others only by boat. Captivating Cane Garden Bay is a favourite stop for yachtsmen in search of local food and dancing at weekends. Beachlife is laid-back, while powerboats, Hobie Cats, kayaks, windsurfers and other water sports equipment are available for hire.

Tranquillity, beauty and relaxation are the bywords at Smuggler's Cove. Setting for the film *The Old Man and the Sea*, it is tucked away at the end of a bumpy road. Little Apple Bay Beach is a haven for surfers and body-boarders who drink at the Bomba Shack by the water's edge before partaking in infamous Full Moon Parties. Secluded down a long, steep road, Brewers Bay attracts snorkellers and scuba divers; lotus-eaters set their watches to island time and enjoy refreshments at the Beach Bar.

A few miles northeast of Tortola, Virgin Gorda is almost two islands, connected by a causeway fringed by Savannah Bay beach. To the south is Spanish Town – also known as the Valley, and Devil's Bay National Park; to the northeast is Virgin Gorda Peak National Park, which rises to 408m (1359ft) then dips down to Gun Creek, where launches meet guests bound for resorts around North Sound.

The island's most famous attraction is the collection of huge granite boulders that are interspersed throughout the northwestern beaches. The Baths, where these boulders, some as much as 12m (40ft) in diameter, create a series of sheltered grottoes and sea pools, contains the most spectacular of these formations.

Six kilometres (4 miles) northwest of Tortola, sleepy Jost Van Dyke retains its traditional West Indian atmosphere. The main village is located along the sandy beach of Great Harbour where there's a number of colourful bars and restaurants that come to life at night. The sheltered lagoon of Little Harbour is popular with sailors and is altogether a more tranquil affair. A multitude of hammocks denotes White Bay to the east and the inimitable Soggy Dollar Bar.

Anegada, or Drowned Land, the only coral atoll in the archipelago, is only 19km (12 miles) long and a couple of miles wide. Ringed by an endless stretch of sand, deserted beaches line the northern and western shores where flocks of

flamingos make their home. Just 8m (28ft) at its highest point, this outcrop is surrounded by a vast horse-shaped barrier reef (the third largest in the world), which throughout the centuries has sent over 300 unsuspecting ships to the deep. The one main village is appropriately called the Settlement.

Privately owned Peter Island, home of a stylish hotel that's ideal for families and honeymooners alike, has two beautiful, palm-fringed beaches in Dead Man's Bay. There are also overnight anchorages in Great Harbour and Little Harbour where turtles can often be seen swimming.

Owned by Richard Branson, Necker Island has a fully staffed mansion perched on the island's summit. All 22 guests are accommodated in the Balinese bamboo and English country pine main house. Millionaires and moguls can sign up for exclusive use of this most prestigious hideaway, 10 minutes by boat from Virgin Gorda.

Salt-water fly fishing might be the fastest-growing sport in the world, but in the BVIs it has been popular for years. The pristine waters, unfished flats and reefs are teeming with Bonefish, Permit and Tarpon. Charter boats in Road Harbour are available for day fishing trips and longer expeditions.

With a cruising area 48km (32 miles) long and half that in width, the BVIs are home to an infinite variety of options, including tacking past The Bight at Norman Island, a leisurely passage to Anegada, an exciting reach past The Dogs, and the treasured realm of the Sir Francis Drake Channel.

The BVIs offer the greatest variety of charter sailing craft in the Caribbean: small sailboats to classic yachts; crewed or bareboat. Easy, deep-water island hops, steady trade winds, line-of-sight navigation and numerous anchorages make this an ideal base for experienced and novice sailors alike. Founded in 1973, the Royal British Virgin Islands Yacht Club in Road Town welcomes visiting yachters.

The most popular and best known of all BVI dive sites is the wreck of the RMS *Rhone*, which sank in 1867. Lying in depths from 6–24m (20–80ft) at Salt Island, this was the setting for the film *The Deep*. With parts of the 95m (310ft) hull still intact, the wreck is colourfully

Left The gigantic boulders at The Baths seem to be strategically arranged by nature to provide hidden beaches, rock pools and trails for the visitor to explore.

Opposite Diving on The Invisibles, near Necker Island, is an experience not to be missed; golden cup corals festoon the massive granite boulders around which legions of fish of every description swirl effortlessly.

decorated by a wide variety of corals and is home to several resident barracuda, sea turtles, stingrays, and angelfish.

Other important sites for divers and snorkellers include Wreck Alley and Thumb Rock off Cooper Island; Alice in Wonderland located in South Bay on Ginger Island; The Indians off Norman Island; Rainbow Canyons at Pelican Island; Painted Walls close by Dead Chest Island; and Treasure Point, believed to have been the inspiration for Robert Louis Stevenson's *Treasure Island*.

Getting married in the BVIs is very popular – no doubt due to the idyllic setting and ease of formalities. Cane Garden Bay, Lambert Bay and Long Bay are traditional favourites, as is the uninhabited islet of Sandy Spit near Jost Van Dyke. Picturesque churches include Mary Star of the Sea Catholic Church, New Life Baptist Church and Zion Hill Methodist Church. Alternatively the world-class hotels on Virgin Gorda and Peter Island are nuptial nirvanas.

It is the siren call of Aeolus that gives this nautical playground its pervasive charm and character. A sibilant sea glistening in the sun and sparkling in the moonlight; distant islands edged by bays of ivory sand beckoning on the horizon. This sequestered pattern of islands exudes an ineffable charm where sophisticated hideaways coexist in perfect harmony with a natural Eden.

Prince Edward Island

PIERRE HOME-DOUGLAS

This is the undiscovered gem of eastern North America. He said it not to boast, but simply as a matter of fact, the testament of a mid-50s father of five who, a few years before, had pulled up stakes in western Massachusetts and moved with his family to Prince Edward Island, off Canada's east coast. He pointed to a nearby bay and a ridge of sand dunes along its northern shore, a narrow spit of land a kilometre or so away. A few hundred metres beyond the dunes lay 10km (6.2 miles) of beach devoid of a single human visitor. In the foreground, a mussel boat chugged its way back to a nearby harbour, a shell's toss away from a wharf-side restaurant that would soon be dishing up the day's catch. 'What's not to love about the place?' he asked. What, indeed?

Prince Edward Island is Canada's smallest province, a crescent-shaped island 224km (139 miles) at its longest point and between six and 64km

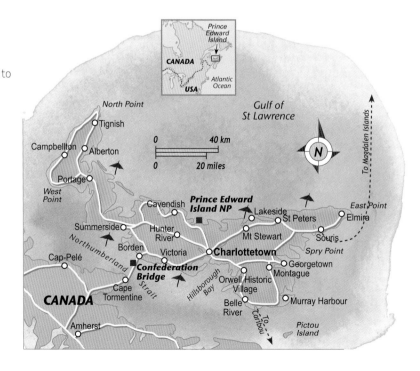

(four and 40 miles) wide. Located in the Gulf of St Lawrence, where it empties into the Atlantic Ocean, Prince Edward Island — PEI to anyone who is familiar with the place — boasts some of the finest, unspoiled beaches in North America. They encircle 5656km² (2184 sq.miles) of gently undulating hills and a rural landscape that seems more 19th Century than 21st. Little wonder that *Travel and Leisure* magazine has named the island North America's best one to visit and one of the top 10 in the world.

The shoreline is publicly owned, meaning that its 805km (500-mile) length is open to anyone wanting to swim, take a stroll, go birdwatching, or just gaze in awe and admiration at the sublime interfaces between land, sea and sky. Road maps of the province show scores of laneways that lead from paved roads down to the shoreline, and small parking areas where you'll spot registration plates from the neighbouring provinces of New Brunswick, Quebec and Ontario, as well as states like Massachusetts in the US Northeast.

Like the plovers and other shorebirds that inhabit the water's edge, most bathers seem to prefer congregating close together as soon as they reach the beach. The lone walker can quickly leave them behind. Passing a bend or two, it's common to look ahead at sand as far as the eye can see, with only sandpipers endlessly scampering in front of you and terns and gulls wheeling overhead to keep you company. Behind you: nothing but footprints.

Unlike Maine and the coastal waters of the rest of the New England states farther south, Prince Edward Island enjoys swimmable waters. Summertime temperatures are roughly 22°C (68°F), the warmest waters north of Virginia, a fortuitous result of the warming current of the Gulf Stream that passes near the island.

For 15,000 years, since the last Ice Age ended and rising water severed it from the mainland, PEI lay untethered to the land it had once joined. This ended in 1997, when the 13km-long (8-mile) Confederation Bridge opened, joining the island to the mainland in New Brunswick across the Northumberland Strait. The imposing one-billion dollar structure caused lots of debate on the island during its conception and construction, not dissimilar to what took place in England with the Channel Tunnel in the late 1980s and early 1990s. Would the bridge fundamentally alter the identity of the island? Would the crime rate rise? Would PEI be inundated by tourists who no longer had to line up for several hours to take the old 40-minute ferry ride?

Happily, the death of the island's bucolic, restful spirit was greatly exaggerated. True, it is far quicker for motorists to reach the island than before — PEI draws a million visitors a year, mostly from eastern Canada and the northeastern United States — but the appeal of the place endures. This is still a province where the majority of people live in rural areas. And the beaches are still, blessedly, largely deserted worlds. Most of them fall into two distinct types. On the north shore, the one facing the Gulf of St Lawrence, the sand is generally light brown and many beaches meander off to the horizon. One stretch, in Prince Edward Island National Park, measures more than 50km (31 miles) long. This is also the shoreline that includes rugged sand dunes, spotted with clumps of Marram grass. In 1998, the Prince Edward Island

Right *The Confederation Bridge links the two Canadian provinces of Prince Edward Island and New Brunswick.*

Opposite *Two beach strollers enjoy the fading light of a summer's day next to the 16th fairway of the Links at Crowbush Golf Course.*

National Park was extended to the east to encompass a 6km-long (4-mile) section, known as the Greenwich dunes, which includes a rare bowl-shaped parabolic dune hundreds of metres wide. To reach the dunes, National Park workers built a 1km (0.6-mile) long walkway that snakes its way through a swamp that is home to great blue herons, bitterns, and ospreys – not to mention the occasional muskrat. The walkway ends at the base of the dunes, where red foxes burrow their dens. A short scramble over a narrow ridge and suddenly the ocean stretches infinitely ahead, and you can imagine yourself much like Keats's 'stout Cortez' when he first gazed in wonder at another ocean – the Pacific – five centuries ago.

The beaches on the south side of Prince Edward Island, facing the Northumberland Strait, are often red sand, a colour that mirrors much of the soil on the island. Drive down any of the numerous unpaved country roads and your car will soon bear witness to the high iron-oxide (rust) content of the soil, with a thin dust-

ing that will survive trips back home a 1000km (621 miles) away. Some parts of the shoreline, like Spry Point near Souris, also feature rugged sandstone cliffs, easier admired from above than by scrambling on the rocky ground below.

Cars offer the most convenient way to get around the island, but this is a land small enough that a bicycle can cover significant distance in a single day. This fact hasn't been lost on the government of the province. In August 2000, it completed the Confederation Trail, which runs from Elmira, near the eastern end of the island, to Tignish, close to its western tip. The 270km (168-mile) path, and its 80km (50 miles) of spur trails, follow an old railway bed that has been replaced with finely crushed gravel. The route is part of the continent-spanning Trans Canada Trail, stretching from the Atlantic to the Pacific oceans. In the wintertime, the trail is taken over by cross-country skiers and snowmobiles. This is, after all, definitely a land of four seasons. The summer months, from early June to late September, are

Above *A raised wooden walkway snakes its way through the marsh behind one of the Greenwich dunes, part of Prince Edward Island National Park.*
Opposite *The Confederation Trail passes by the town of St Peters, where mussel nets dot the harbour.*

the most popular time to visit the island, when temperatures during the daytime typically reach a comfortable mid-20°C (68°F). Wintertime can see temperatures plunge below 0°C (32°F), and snow heavy enough to isolate rural towns.

Recent years have seen a sharp growth in first-rate golf courses on the island. Perhaps the most celebrated course is the Links at Crowbush, near Lakeside, on the north shore. Designed by renowned golf architect Thomas McBroom, the Scottish links-style course was artfully crafted to meld with the landscape of the area, with the seashore never far from sight. Hit an errant tee shot on the 16th hole and you might end up trying to find your ball on the beach before high tide rolls in. Crowbush was voted Canada's best new public course when it opened in 1994, and still consistently ranks in the top 10. But this is more than just a playground by the sea. PEI is still a rural world. More than half of its 140,000 residents live in the countryside.

That fact is reflected in large fields of clover and potatoes – an island mainstay, quiet back roads, and places like Victoria-by-the-Sea on the south shore. True, the town caters to tourists in the summer, with a chocolate shop, candle store, and a fine used bookstore housed in an old barn. No flashy neon signs or billboards. This is a town where people actually live and work, and a stroll down any of the side streets testifies to its peaceful, lived-in feeling.

The Orient Hotel in the town has been welcoming guests for more than a century, sometimes former residents. After all, the island seems to exert a homing effect on its progeny. Many of its residents leave the island in their early adult years, seeking opportunities in other areas of Canada – the cities of Ontario or the vast western provinces. But many of them end up coming back to retire. This seems to be one place where you can go home again.

Visitor or resident, many are drawn to summertime get-togethers for musicians that occur in scores of towns across the province. Known by the Gaelic word *ceilidh* (pronounced kay-lee), or just plain 'shindig', these lively affairs typically include guitarists and fiddle players. Some invite people to get up from the audience and bang out a tune on a piano, strum a borrowed guitar, or even tell a story or two. The 'grand-daddy' of them all takes place every Wednesday night at Orwell

Historic Village, a collection of buildings from the mid to the late 19th century, including a schoolhouse, general store, church, and an old meeting hall where the weekly ceilidh takes place.

The history of the island goes back a lot further than Orwell Village. PEI has been home to humans for 10,000 years. It was originally called Abegweit, or 'cradled in the waves', by its first residents, the native Indians known as the Mi'kmaq (pronounced Mic-mac). The first white man to lay eyes on it was the French explorer Jacques Cartier in 1534, who reported that it was 'The finest land 'tis possible to see. Full of fine meadows and trees.' The French claimed the land they named Isle St Jean, and held control for more than two centuries until British troops captured it in 1745. Three years later, the island was traded back to the French in exchange for a city in India. But the new French rule was short-lived. The Seven-Years War, carried on in both Europe and North America, ended with the defeat of the French in 1763. As part of the Treaty of Paris, the French ceded Isle St Jean to the British, who later renamed the island in honour of King George III's son, Prince Edward, the future father of Queen Victoria.

The island played a role far beyond its size in the formation of Canada, for it was here, in the capital city of Charlottetown in 1864, that political leaders arrived from the British North America colonies to discuss a union. The meeting led to a follow-up conference in Quebec the same year and, in 1867, to

Above left The home that provided the setting for Prince Edward Island's most famous fictional heroine, *Anne of Green Gables*, draws visitors from around the world.

Left A stack of lobster pots lies ready for use in Victoria-by-the-sea.

Opposite The typical red earth of Prince Edward Island is fertile ground for the province's most famous crop – potatoes.

the founding of Canada. Ironically, PEI was not one of the four first provinces; islanders were initially fine with joining the Confederation which only came in six years later. Today, the room where the Fathers of Confederation met in Province House is preserved as a National Historic Site.

Still, the most famous PEI resident was not a politician, but a feisty red-haired girl, Anne of Green Gables. Mark Twain called her 'the most delightful child hero-ine since the Immortal Alice (of *Alice in Wonderland*). Anne was the creation of PEI native Lucy Maud Montgomery. Her 1908 novel has been reprinted in more than 40 languages, and has spawned films, television series and a whole tourism indus-try. It's difficult to travel anywhere on the island without seeing Anne's visage peering back at you from coffee mugs, T-shirts, and hundreds of other products – even some car registration plates. Her story was transformed into a

musical which has been running every summer since 1965 at Charlottetown's popular Confederation Centre of the Arts. Ground Zero for the Anne industry is the Green Gables house itself, located near the north shore town of Cavendish. Readers of the Anne books – *Anne of Green Gables* was only the first in a series of more than a dozen books that revolve around her growth to adulthood – would instantly rec-ognize the white-clapboard, green-trimmed home. Less familiar would be the gift shop, large parking lot, and droves of tourists who descend on the site.

But in true PEI 'fashion', Cavendish is an anomaly. Drive a few miles away from here, turn down a small country road, and you are back in the PEI that seemingly defies time. There's a lobster fisherman coming back to port, a farmer wrapping hay into large bundles in a field, or school children wandering down a red dirt road to a beach. Suddenly you're back in the real Prince Edward Island, and you are home.

Kauai

DOUG PERRINE

hat kind of a place is this island with the funny name? Is it a rainforest, a desert or a swamp? A land of rugged inhospitable mountains and craggy canyons? Or one of gentle agricultural plains and inviting white sand beaches? Some uncertainty is understandable, considering that people can't even agree on how to pronounce the name. Most people use two syllables, with the accent on the second: ka WYE. However, the proper enunciation of this Hawaiian name would be in three syllables: 'ka WA' ee.'

As to the original questions, the answer is 'all of the above'. Hawaii's unique topography and weather patterns produce a range of landscapes and climatic conditions which are unparalleled for the amount of diversity within a very small area. Kauai, the northwestern-most of the main Hawaiian Islands, sits just below the Tropic of Cancer in the central Pacific, roughly one-third of the way

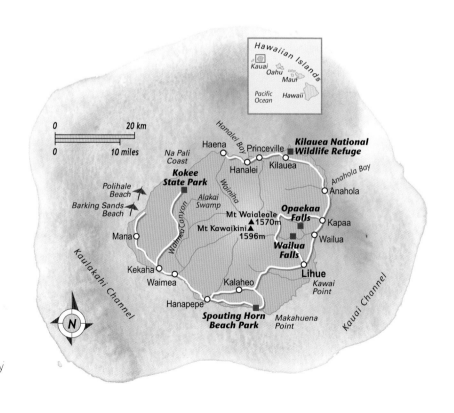

from California to China. Its tropical, oceanic location ensures that the average differences in weather from month to month are fairly minimal. However, the differences from place to place on an island of only 1438km^2 (553sq.miles) can be astounding. The steep, high mountains, thrusting over 1500m (5000ft) above sea level, force the consistent trade winds upward, causing the air to cool rapidly and lose its moisture, which falls abundantly on the windward slopes, especially at high elevations. The leeward parts of the island are left in the 'rain shadow'. The resulting microclimate zones are both extremely different and very close to each other. The top of Mt Waialeale is one of the two wettest places on earth, receiving about 11.5m (450in) of rain each year. Only about 28km (17 miles) away, Barking Sands Beach is kissed by a mere 20cm (8in) of rain per year.

It's perhaps more interesting to consider the kind of people who go to Kauai. Devotees of 'high culture' will be disappointed with the distinct lack of opera houses, symphonies, stage musicals, art museums, and other trappings of European civilization. Nature lovers and adventure hunters, however, flock to this place.

Kauai is uniquely attractive to one particular group of vacationers: honeymooners. Hawaii as a whole hosts a lot of newlyweds, and wedding ceremonies, but a dispro-portionate number of these blissful couples go to Kauai. Why? Perhaps it's all the rain. As we all know, there's not a lot to do outdoors when it's raining. To be sure, not all parts of the island receive a lot of rainfall. But virtually all visitor accommodations are located in areas that get enough rainfall to keep them green. These same areas also get a lot of sunshine. While grey clouds may pile up on the mountain peaks and it drizzles for hours, coastal areas tend to get passing showers that are quickly followed by blue skies, brilliant sunshine, and often rainbows.

The frequent showers and abundant sunshine fuel a lush growth of vegetation that produces a sort of 'Garden of Eden' effect that may inspire loving couples to imagine themselves as Adam and Eve in their primeval paradise. The tropical jungle, waterfalls, sunny beaches and misty mountainous interior all conspire to summon up a fantasy picture of a storybook earth in its untouched innocence. But wait – it's more than that. There is a distinct sense of *déjà vu* – a feeling that you've actually been here before. In a sense you have – at least if you've been to the movies. Kauai has been a favourite setting for film producers since the 1930s, and has been used as a location for over 60 films and television series, including *South Pacific, King Kong, Raiders of the Lost Ark, Fantasy Island, Gilligan's Island,* and *Jurassic Park.* Whenever Hollywood needs to conjure up a fantasy location that is

Right *The roadless Na Pali coast, along the northwest shore of Kauai, is sliced by impossibly steep valleys separated by knife-edge ridges.*

Opposite *Kalalau lookout in Kokee State Park, presents a view of Kalalau Valley that has to be one of the most stunning vistas in the world.*

extraordinarily romantic, mysterious and exotic, the production team heads to Kauai.

Not every island has its own colour scheme, but Kauai is distinctly green and red. These are contrasted with the deep cobalt blue of the tropical sky and sea, and accented with the myriad other hues. But when you look to the land, what you see is primarily a duo-tone pattern of intensely green vegetation splattered across a backdrop of deep rust-red volcanic soil. The rusty colour of the soil is due to iron oxides (rust) in the volcanic ash. The propensity of Kauai mud to permanently stain anything that touches it was considered a curse until a clever local entrepreneur decided to market soiled laundry as 'red dirt T-shirts'. The earth-coloured garments were a sensation, and overnight the soil became 'red gold'.

The geological history of Kauai is on display in layers of varying shades of green and red (due partly to the varying iron content in the assorted eruptions that formed the island) at Waimea Canyon, often referred to as the 'Grand Canyon of the Pacific'. Although much smaller than the Grand Canyon, it is large enough to be quite impressive and is arguably more colourful and attractive than the Grand Canyon itself. There are several lookouts over Waimea Canyon on the road up to Kokee State Park, where lookouts into the island's signature attraction can be found. This is Kalalau Valley, the largest valley on Kauai's Na Pali Coast. The Na Pali is a section of the northwestern coastline of Kauai that has been eroded into such rugged topography that it is impossible to build a road around this part of the island. The valleys are separated by razorback ridges that seem impossibly thin and rise near-vertically over 1000m (3300ft) from the valley floor to the crenellated ridges, which are so jagged that it gives you goose bumps to see goats walking on them. The topography is similar to the islands of Bora Bora and Moorea in French Polynesia, but more extreme.

The entire Na Pali Coast can be seen from the air, by helicopter tour, or from the sea by 'raft' (inflatable pontoon boat) or boat tour. Kalalau Valley can also be reached by an 18km (11 mile) hike, each way, which typically requires four to six days return. The hike is challenging and requires a camping permit. More visitors opt to hike only the first 3km (2 miles) of the trail into Hanakapiai Valley which, although not as spectacular as Kalalau, has a nice beach as well as a 120m-high (400ft) waterfall, with a nice swimming hole in the back. The waterfall is an additional 3km (2 miles) of hiking each way from the beach.

For hikers who prefer higher elevations and cooler temperatures, the Pihea Trail in Kokee State Park skirts the rear rim of Kalalau Valley at an elevation of 1040m (3400ft), offering dizzying views into the valley, before it cuts back through the Alakai swamp, with its weird stunted vegetation. The Alakai is touted as the highest swamp in the world. Much of the world-record rainfall that dumps on Mt Waialeale flows through the Alakai before descending via sheer waterfalls into five major rivers, three of which carved out Waimea Canyon.

For those who would like the spectacular views and fresh air without all the hiking, there are sunrise and sunset downhill bicycle tours that start at Waimea Canyon and descend to the coast

Above *Queen's Bath, off Kapiolani Road in Princeville, on Kauai's north shore, is an idyllic tidal pool on a rocky section of coastline.*

Opposite *At the end of the hike from the beach to Hanakapiai Valley is a magnificent waterfall that plunges into a refreshing natural swimming pool.*

over a three- to four-hour period, with almost no pedaling required. Three of Kauai's rivers can be explored by kayak, canoe or boat. Some freshwater areas have been stocked with bass and trout for anglers, while saltwater fishing enthusiasts can find marlin, tuna, wahoo, and dorado or mahi-mahi in the offshore waters.

Kauai's lush vegetation has led tourism officials to dub it the 'Garden Island'. Fittingly, there are a number of excellent botanical gardens and arboretums. In stark contrast, the scenery at Polihale Beach on the western end of the island is more akin to the Sahara Desert, with sand piled up in dunes up to 30m (100ft) high. The road ends here, but the beach goes on for another 27km (17 miles). This is a big part

of the allure of Kauai. There are parts of it that you can only get to by walking, crawling, paddling, or falling. There are places that are hidden, places that are wild, places that are dangerous, mysterious, and full of the history of vanished peoples. Even the rugged Na Pali Coast was once inhabited by hundreds of thousands of Hawaiians. Before the Hawaiians arrived, roughly 1000 years ago, an enigmatic race known as the 'Menehune' ruled the land. Anthropologists still debate the identity and even the existence of these people, but they have left behind more evidence on Kauai than on the other Hawaiian Islands.

All of the Hawaiian Islands have roadless sections and spectacular scenery, but nowhere is a view as likely to provoke a breathless 'I can't believe what I'm seeing!' as on Kauai. This is because Kauai is both the wettest and the oldest of the Hawaiian islands. Consequently it has suffered the most extreme and dramatic erosion, and has a greater concentration of waterfalls. Helicopter tours generally end with a grand finale at Waialeale Crater, where a vertical mountainside, appropriately known as the 'Weeping Wall', can sprout so many waterfalls after a good rain that they are as uncountable as the hairs on the head of a Hawaiian goddess.

By no means is a helicopter or hike required to see waterfalls on Kauai. There are drive-up lookouts for the impressive 52m (170ft) Wailua Falls and 46m (150ft) Opaekaa Falls. To see water blasting in the opposite direction in defiance of gravity, stop at Spouting Horn Beach Park on the south shore. Here ocean swells compress air and seawater into a chamber under the lava beach shelf until it spurts like a geyser out of an opening on top of the shelf. Another opening next to it produces the hair-raising sound effects – said by Hawaiians to be the roar of a giant sacred lizard. The magnitude of the display depends upon tide, swell size, and other factors.

Kauai is also unique among the Hawaiian islands in not having suffered the introduction of the mongoose, a small predatory mammal from India that has caused the extirpation of some native birds from the other islands. As a result, there are a number of rare and endemic native birds that can be found only on Kauai. The most ubiquitous member of the avian fauna is the red jungle fowl – an ancestor of the domestic chicken. These were brought to Hawaii by the original Polynesian settlers, and escaped into the bush where they began to breed on their own. The endemic Hawaiian goose, or nene (NAY nay), can also be encountered all around the island, while the smaller native birds require spending some serious time in the rain forest, preferably with an expert guide. Kilauea National Wildlife Refuge, on the north shore, hosts breeding seabirds, including albatrosses, in season.

Kauai is also a good place to see endemic Hawaiian plants, and over a quarter of the fish on Kauai's reefs cannot be found outside of Hawaii. A mere 40 x 53km (25 x 33 miles) in extent, Kauai packs a tremendous amount of diversity and hidden treasures into a small area. Yes, Kauai is for lovers, but it is also for anyone with a love of nature and an adventurous spirit to match.

Right *One of the most dramatic views of the Na Pali coastal mountains on the island of Kauai is from Princeville. This view at sunset hints at their breathtaking beauty.*

Directory information

AEOLIAN ISLANDS

Best time to go: May to October

Contact: Carasco Hotel, Porto delle Genti, Lipari, Italy

Tel: +39 (090) 981 1605

Fax: +39 (090) 981 1828

E-mail: info@carasco.com

Websites: www.carasco.com/english

Activities: walking, hiking, volcanoes, hot springs, watersports, dancing, cycling, scooter excursions, horse riding, tennis, boat cruises.

CORSICA

Best time to go: May to September

Contact: Agence de Tourisme de la Corse;
17 Blvd du Roi Jérôme, Ajaccio, Corse

Tel: +33 (049) 551 0000

E-mail: info@visit-corsica.com

Website: www.visit-corsica.com

Activities: watersports, skiing, 4x4 safaris, climbing, hiking, horse riding, paragliding, tree trail.

CAPRI

Best time to go: May to November

Contact: Piazzetta I Cerio, 11

Tel: +39 (081) 837 5308

Fax: +39 (081) 837 0918

E-mail: information@capri.it

Website: www.capritourism.com

Activities: watersports, spas, museums, caves, ancient ruins, dining, shopping, outdoor activities.

KORCULA

Best time to go: May and September

Contact: Korcula Tourism Office

Tel: +38 (520) 715 701

Fax: +38 (520) 715 866

E-mail: info@korculainfo.com

Website: www.korculainfo.com

Activities: watersports, hiking, fishing, fitness clubs.

BELLE-ÎLE

Best time to go: November to March

Contact: Office de Tourisme de Belle-Île en Mer, Quai Bonnelle, BP 30, 56360 Le Palais

Tel: +33 (029) 731 8193

Fax: +33 (029) 731 5617

E-mail: found on the website below

Website: www.belle-ile.com

Activities: walking, cycling, sailing, horse riding, marinas, aerodome, golf, tennis, equestrian centres, watersports, thalassotherapy centre.

RHODES

Best time to go: November to March

Contact: Rodos Hotels Association

Tel/Fax: +30 (241) 77 555

E-mail: hotelsassoc@rho.forthnet.gr

Website: www.RodosIsland.gr

Activities: watersports, museums, cultural events, art galleries, nightlife, aquarium, casino, walking, shopping, winery, medieval sites.

SANTORINI

Best time to go: May to September

Contact: Heliowebs, Ypsilantou 28, GR-172 36, Dafni, Athens

Tel: +30 (210) 973 0697

Fax: +30 (210) 976 7208

E-mail: info@heliowebs.gr

Website: www. santorini.net

Activities: museums, walks, nightlife, sightseeing, snorkelling, volcano day trips.

MALTA

Best time to go: February to October

Contact address: Malta Tourism Authority; Merchants Street, Valletta (MR 02)

London SW18 1DD

Tel: +356 (2) 291 5800

Fax: +356 (2) 291 5893

E-mail: info@visitmalta.com

Website: www.visitmalta.com

Activities: diving, beaches, walking, rock climbing.

RÜGEN

Best time to go: June to September

Contact: Tourismuszentrale Rügen, Markt 4, D-18528 Bergen auf Rügen

Tel: +49 (383) 880 770

Fax: +49 (383) 825 4440

E-mail: info@ruegen.de

Website: www.ruegen.de

Activities: Rügensche Kleinbahn railway journey, theatre, museums, watersports, outdoor activities.

GOTLAND

Best time to go: May to August

Contact: Gotlands Turistförening, Hamngatan 4, Box 1403, 62153 Visby

Tel: +46 (049) 827 1300

Fax: +46 (049) 821 1746

E-mail: info@mail.gotland.net

Website: www.gotland.net

Activities: horse riding, hiking, fishing, mountain biking, golf, diving, caving, watersports, shooting, motorsports, arts, museums, theatres, spas.

MALDIVES

Best time to go: December to April

Contact: Maldives Tourism Promotion Board, 12 Boduthakurufaanu Magu, Malé, Republic of Maldives

Tel +60 323 228

Fax +60 323 229

E-mail: mtpb@visitmaldives.com

Website: www.visitmaldives.com

Activities: scuba diving, snorkelling, submarines, surfing, fishing, cruise ships.

MAURITIUS

Best time to go: All year round

Contact: Website provides contacts for the tourism offices of Mauritius in South Africa, Germany, the UK, Italy, France, India, Switzerland and Austria.

E-mail: found on the website below

Website: www.mauritius.net

Activities: golf, markets, deep sea fishing, festivities, shopping, spas, climbing, walking, hiking, caving, biking, watersports, nightlife, undersea walks, snorkelling.

RÉUNION

Best time to go: April to October

Contact: Website provides contacts for the tourism offices of the North, South, East, West, High Plains and Cirques.

E-mail: found on the website below

Website: www.la-reunion-tourisme.com

Activities: hiking, horse riding, 4x4, climbing, cycling, airsports, golf, watersports, parachuting, gardens and museums.

ZANZIBAR

Best time to go: July to October

Contact: Tour operators listed on the website.

E-mail: found on the website below

Website: www.zanzibar.net

Activities: diving, snorkelling, deep sea fishing, sailing, architecture.

BALI

Best time to go: April to mid-November

Contact: Bali.com Ltd, Reservation and Service Centre.

Tel: +62 (361) 703 060

Fax: +62 (361) 701 577

E-mail: info@bali.com

Website: www.bali.com

Activities: watersports, spas, diving, game fishing, boat cruises, golf, tennis, squash, paragliding, whitewater rafting, bungy jumping, horse riding, nature tours.

LORD HOWE ISLAND

Best time to go: All year round

Contact: Lord Howe Island Visitor Centre – website provides contact numbers.

E-mail: lhi.visitorcentre@bigpond.com

Website: www.lordhoweisland.info

Activities: golf, tennis, bowls, watersports, hand-feeding fish, glass bottom boat trips, fishing cruises, bird watching, cycling, hiking and climbing.

FIJI

Best time to go: All year round

Contact: Head Office of Fiji Visitors Bureau,

Suite 107, Colonial Plaza, Namaka, Nadi

Tel: + (679) 672 2433

Fax: + (679) 672 0141

E-mail: infodesk@bulafiji.com

Website: www.bulafiji.com

Activities: watersports, fishing, hiking, golf, shopping,

cruising and charters, bird watching, safaris.

BORA BORA

Best time to go: May to October

Contact: Bora Bora Visitors Bureau:

P.O. Box 144- 98 730 Vaitape- Bora Bora

Tel/Fax: + 689 677 636

E-mail: webmaster@boraboraisland.com

Website: www.boraboraisland.com/tours.html

Activities: watersports, 4x4 safaris, arts and crafts,

shopping and dining, lagoon exploration, breakfast

by canoe, shark and ray feeding, hiking,

horse riding, spas.

GRENADA

Best time to go: December to May

Contact: Grenada Board of Tourism, Burns Point,

P.O. Box 293, St George's, Grenada

Tel: +14 (73) 440 2279

Fax: +14 (73) 440 6637

E-mail: gbt@caribsurf.com

Website: www.grenadagrenadines.com

Activities: hiking, mountain biking, bird watching,

recreational sports, sightseeing, historical sites,

shopping.

BRITISH VIRGIN ISLANDS

Best time to go: All year round

Contact: B.V.I. Tourist Board, P.O. Box 134, Road Town,

Tortola. B.V.I.

Tel: +1284 494 3134

Fax: +1284 494 3866

E-mail: info@bvitouristboard.com

Website: www.bvitourism.com

Activities: carnival and festivals, regattas, sightseeing,

watersports, scuba diving, fishing, spectator sports, arts

and crafts.

MARTINIQUE

Best time to go: All year round

Contact: Comité Martiniquais du Tourisme,

Immeuble Le Beaupré, Pointe de Jaham,

97233 Schoelcher Martinique. F.W.I.

Tel: +596 616 177

Fax: +596 612 272

E-mail: info@martinique.org

Website: www.martinique.org

Activities: tennis, golf, watersports, hiking, mountain

biking, ultra-light aircraft, horse riding, festivals,

carnivals.

KAUAI, HAWAII

Best time to go: All year round

Contact: 4334 Rice Street, Suite 101,

Lihu'e, HI 96766

Tel: +1808 245 3971 or +1800 262 1400 (toll-free)

North America

Fax: +1808 246 9235

E-mail: khvq@kauai-hawaii.com

Website: www.kauai-hawaii.com

Activities: golf, fishing, hiking, horse riding, watersports.

Right *The view at sunrise from Bali's Mt Batur of Lake Batur, Mt Abang and Mt Agung, engenders all the emotions of awe and serenity we associate with the most beautiful islands of the world.*

Previous page *As the visitor approaches the turquoise waters of Mnemba Reef, Unguja (Zanzibar) Tanzania, sea and sky blend in an ocean of blue; the island's clear waters and abundant marine life make it a top dive destination.*

The Authors

ANTHONY LAMBERT has written or contributed to eight travel books, including three *Insight* guides, and is a frequent contributor to the South African Independent Newspapers group's highly regarded travel section. He has also written articles for such newspapers and magazines as the *New York Times*, *Daily Telegraph*, *Financial Times*, *Orient-Express Magazine* and *Wanderlust*. He works part-time for the National Trust, Europe's largest conservation organisation and has lectured to a wide variety of audiences, including the Royal Geographical Society, of which he is a Fellow.

Freelance journalist BRIAN RICHARDS has been a regular visitor to Malta for the past 25 years, returning year after year and cultivating an interest in the country's history and culture while witnessing the great changes in one of the UK's favourite holiday destinations. He has contributed articles on the Maltese islands on an ongoing basis to the trade and consumer press in the UK – including *ABTA Magazine*, *Travel Weekly* and *Classic Travel* – and is the author of a number of guide books, including the *Globetrotter Travel Guide to Malta*.

DOUG PERRINE, a resident of Kailua-Kona, Hawaii, is widely regarded as one of the world's foremost marine wildlife photographers. His award-winning photographs have been published in hundreds of books, calendars, posters, postcards, and other graphic products, and thousands of magazines. He is also an accomplished author, with seven books and hundreds of magazine articles to his credit. His academic credentials include B.S. and M.A. degrees in marine biology. He is the founder of the stock photo library SeaPics.com, which he operated for 18 years before selling it in 2003 to concentrate on his own writing and photography.

FIONA MCINTOSH is the author of *Seven Days in Mauritius* (published by Struik Publishers) and the editor of the South African-based *Out There Adventure and Travel Guides* and *Divestyle Magazine*. Southern Africa and the Indian Ocean islands are her specialty and she has contributed to various New Holland Publishers titles on diving and hiking in the region.

FIONA NICHOLS lived in Italy many years ago and has remained an ardent Italophile ever since, seizing any opportunity to revisit its architecture, museums, restaurants and its unspoilt shores. She has photographed and written hundreds of travel and lifestyle articles over the years for European, Asian and African publications, and has penned a number of *Globetrotter Guides*, including *Globetrotter Guide to Sicily* – where she fell under the charms of the Aeolian islands. Currently based near the Spanish border in the south of France, she continues to travel, photograph and write for publications worldwide

GARY BUCHANAN has been a specialist travel writer for over 20 years. He is a frequent visitor to the Caribbean and enjoys 'collecting' islands. His great love is cruising, which has taken him to the four corners of the globe. He is a former chairman of the British Guild of Travel Writers; Fellow of the Royal Geographical Society; and Fellow of the Institute of Travel & Tourism. Scottish-born, he has written five books and contributes to several national newspapers in Britain.

GRAHAM MERCER is English but has lived for almost 30 years in Dar es Salaam, where he taught at the International School of Tanganyika. He now works as a writer/photographer and has published eight books, and is currently writing and helping to illustrate new guide books to Tanzania's national parks. Graham spends much of his time on safari but has always been fascinated by Zanzibar, especially its historic Stone Town. In 1964, when he was a young sailor in the Royal Navy, his ship was the first to arrive in Zanzibar during the revolution which overthrew the last Omani sultan. He is a Fellow of the Royal Geographic Society and a member of International MENSA.

GRAHAM SIMMONS is a freelance travel writer/photographer based in Byron Bay, Australia. He started travel writing in 1993, in an effort to find meaning 'out there'. He says, 'travel is a cure for which there is no known disease. As people start to travel more and really get to understand one another, war and conflict will become things of the past'. Graham is a full member of the Australian Society of Travel Writers and is the founding member of the Global Travel Writer's Syndicate.

PIERRE HOME-DOUGLAS has worked as a freelance travel writer for more than 20 years. His articles have appeared in numerous Canadian and American newspapers and magazines on subjects including cycling through Vermont, hiking in England, canoeing in Canada, and sailing up the Nile. He has written chapters for travel books, including New Holland Publishers' *The World's Great Railway Journeys*, the *Eyewitness Guide to New England*, and Reader's Digest's *Explore America* series. He lives in Montreal, where he has also worked as a college professor and a book editor for St Remy Press.

PHILIP GAME His independent travels began in the 1960s in Tasmania and have included a year-long odyssey hitch-hiking across Eurasia as well a stint as an adventure tour guide in Southeast Asia. Later, he and his wife Barbara survived 13 months branded as 'resident aliens' in small-town Pennsylvania and then dodged Britain's remorseless television licence inspectors for six months. Philip's career as a freelance travel writer based in Melbourne, Australia has seen him locked in the medieval town hall tower of Tallinn, Estonia and stranded by monsoon rains in rural Malaysia. His work has been published in 33 countries.

Scottish-born ROBIN GAULDIE first visited the Greek islands more than 30 years ago and has been exploring the Aegean and Ionian isles ever since – though there are still a few remote dots on the map that he has not yet visited. He is the author of several travel guides to the islands and mainland Greece, and to other travel destinations around the world. When not island-hopping, he divides his time between Edinburgh and his house in a village in southern France.

ROBIN MCKELVIE has harboured a love of islands since his parents took him to the same idyllic Scottish island (Arran) every summer as a child. Since 1997 Robin has been working full time as a travel writer and photographer, and his trips have taken him to over 70 countries and over 50 islands. In addition to writing for UK, US and Australian magazines and newspapers, Robin has also written books on his native Scotland as well as Croatia and Slovenia.

RODNEY BOLT first visited Madeira in 1994, and immediately fell in love with the island. He has been going back there every year. That early visit produced the first comprehensive travel guide to Madeira to be published in decades – a book now joined by many others, as the island surges in popularity. Bolt lives in Amsterdam in the Netherlands, has written a number of other travel guides, and contributes frequently to food and travel publications around the world. His first work of fiction, an imagined biography of the spy and playwright Christopher Marlowe, was published in 2004.

Editor of *Holiday & Leisure* magazine and one of Britain's most experienced travel writers, ROGER ST PIERRE has visited 117 countries around the globe and has a special penchant for islands. A published writer since the age of 15, he is the author of more than 30 books, as well as articles for such publications as *Incentive Travel*, *Independent Travel Trade News*, *Short Breaks Worldwide*, the *Times Business Supplement* and *Essentially America*. Roger is a long-time member of the prestigious British Guild Of Travel Writers and an Honourary Colonel of the Commonwealth of Kentucky.

After an academic career, ROWLAND MEAD has been a full-time writer for over a decade. He writes on wildlife and travel topics and his books include the *Globetrotter Guides* to Costa Rica, Iceland, Milan and the Italian Lakes, Tenerife, Gran Canaria and Lanzarote, as well as two volumes on English cathedral cities. He has also contributed numerous articles to wildlife and travel magazines. Rowland is an accomplished artist, working mainly in acrylics, and has had many of his paintings exhibited, while his line drawings illustrate a number of his books. Rowland lives in south Devon, England.

It's hard to say which was the pivotal moment of WILLIAM GRAY'S travelling career – surviving the first long-haul flight with his toddler twins or clinching the coveted Travel Writer of the Year award in 2002. A regular contributor to *The Sunday Times* and the family travel columnist for *Wanderlust* magazine, he has also written guidebooks (both published by New Holland Publishers) on Athens and Zambia. At the age of 23, his first book, *Coral Reefs & Islands: The Natural History of a Threatened Paradise* was highly commended in the Conservation Book Prize. A member of the British Guild of Travel Writers, William's idea of the perfect island is anywhere remote with plenty of seabirds.

ZOE ROSS has worked as a travel editor of guidebooks for the past eight years as well as being a travel writer and journalist for a number of publishers and national newspapers. She lives in London, but spends a large portion of each year in southern France.

Photographic acknowledgements

Abbreviations to photographer's names below: JH = Johanna Huber; BA = Biscaro Allesandro; GS = Giovanni Simeone; FO = Fantuz Olimpio; SA = Saffo Allesandro; GS = Giovanni Simeone; RM = Ripani Masimo; DR = D. Rogers; RR = Rinaldi Roberto; GA = Gampicollo Angelo; GM = Gideon Mendel.

cover		Gallo Images/gettyimages.com	49	left	RM/Sime/Photo Access	111		Fiona Mcintosh
back cover		JH/Sime/Photo Access	49	right	International Photobank	112		Gallo Images/gettyimages.com
cover flap		International Photobank	50		International Photobank	113		Travelink/David Forman
end paper		Shaen Adey	51–52		Photo Access	114		Photo Access
1		JH/Sime/Photo Access	53–55		International Photobank	115	left	Paul Miles
2-3		Travel Library	56		GS/Sime/Photo Access	115	right	GA/Sime/Photo Access
4-5		Shaen Adey	57		GS/Sime/Photo Access	116		Graham Simmons
6-7		JH/Sime/Photo Access	58–59		Roger St Pierre	117		FLPA/C. Marshall
8		Travel Library	60–61		GS/Sime/Photo Access	118		Travel Library
11		JH/Sime/Photo Access	62–63		International Photobank	119		Donna Carol/Travel Stock
12-13		Terry Harris	64		Travelink/David Foreman			Photography
14		BA/Sime/Photo Access	65	top	Travel Library	120	left	Michael AW
15		GS/Sime/Photo Access	65	below	International Photobank	121–122		Travel Library
16	top	GS/Sime/Photo Access	66		Paul Harris	123		Donna Carol/Travel Stock
16	below	Travel Library	67		Dennis Hardley			Photography
17-18		JH/Sime/Photo Access	68		FO/Sime/Photo Access	124–125		Travel Library
19	top	FLPA/T. Micak	69		Dennis Hardley	126–127		International Photobank
19	below	JH/Sime/Photo Access	70–71		Paul Harris	128	top	Photo Access
20		JH/Sime/Photo Access	72		Anthony J Lambert	128	below	Terry Harris
21-23		Fiona Nichols	73		Frank Niebauer	129		International Photobank
24		JH/Sime/Photo Access	74–75		Anthony J Lambert	130		David Sanger
25		FO/Sime/Photo Access	77		FLPA/Silvestris	131		Photo Access
26		William Gray	78–81		Anders Tuckler	132		David Sanger
27-28		FO/Sime/Photo Access	82–83		William Gray	133–134		International Photobank
29		International Photobank	84		Axiom	135		Photo Access
30		FO/Sime/Photo Access	85		Photo Access	136		Terry Harris
31		Robin McKelvie	86		DR/Getaway/Photo Access	137		International Photobank
32		FO/Sime/Photo Access	87	top	DR/Getaway/Photo Access	138		JH/Sime/Photo Access
33	top	Robin McKelvie	87	below	RR/Sime/Photo Access	139		Terry Harris
33	below	International Photobank	88–89		International Photobank	140		Travel Library
34		International Photobank	90–93		Shaen Adey	141		Lawson Wood
35		SA/Sime/Photo Access	94		Fiona McIntosh	142		Pierre Home-Douglas
36		Travel Library	95		FLPA/A. Van Zandbergen	143		Buddy Mays/Travel Stock
37	left	SA/Sime/Photo Access	96–97		Fiona McIntosh			Photography
37	right	International Photobank	98		Photo Access	144–146		Pierre Home-Douglas
38		JH/Sime/Photo Access	99		GM-South Photographic/	147		Buddy Mays/Travel Stock
39		International Photobank			africapictures.net			Photography
40		GS/Sime/Photo Access	100		Tamlyn Beaumont-Thomas	148		GS/Sime/Photo Access
41	top	GS/Sime/Photo Access	101		William Gray	149		Buddy Mays/Travel Stock
41	below	Travel Library	102–103		Travel Library			Photography
42-43		GS/Sime/Photo Access	104–105		International Photobank	150		FLPA/M. Newman
44		Travel Library	106	top	International Photobank	151		GS/Sime/Photo Access
45	top	International Photobank	106	below	Nigel Hicks	152–153		Buddy Mays/Travel Stock
45	below	Peter Wilson	107		Nigel Hicks			Photography
46		Travelink/Alan Bedding	108		Philip Game	154		William Gray
47		Terry Harris	109		Fiona McIntosh	157		Nigel Hicks
48		Travel Library	110		Philip Game	158–59		JH/Sime/Photo Access